The
ANNALS
of a
CENTURY

BRIDGEMAN'S OF LICHFIELD

1878 - 1978

by

OWEN KEYTE

ಜೊ

᚛ଈୢ୫᚜

THE ANNALS OF A CENTURY

ISBN 0 905985 06 0

Printed by N A Tector Ltd, Aldridge
Typographical design and typesetting by
Digital Images, Walsall

᚛ଈୢ୫᚜

CREB

CONTENTS

CREB

PREFACE

A family of English yeomen, settled for many generations in the Fen district of Cambridgeshire, is claimed as the ancestry of the principal character described in the following account.

Left an orphan at the age of 5½ to be brought up by a great uncle, William by name, the early history of the man whose prowess will be narrated remains obscure, the day and year of birth being a subject of some doubt, though thought to have been September 12 within the years 1842-44. It is known however that he was born at Burwell and that Robert was chosen as his Christian name, presumably after the Robert Bridgeman described as Feoffee of ecclesiastical estates and Churchwarden of Burwell Church near Cambridge from 1709 to 1723.

With more certainty the boy can be assumed an artistic temperament, and though in early youth was sent to Thetford to be employed for several years at the engineering works of Charles Burrell, it may be that here, as an addition to mechanical knowledge, an insight into the handling of woodworking tools was gained, intricately carved equipment possibly being executed there as a complement to the big showman's engines for which the firm afterwards became famous. If so, this might be considered a useful preliminary to his later apprenticeship at the business of Messrs. Rattee and Kett of Cambridge where, in the ecclesiastical sphere, his ability to carve in wood and stone was developed, and that he was well able to apply pencil to paper in the production of detail drawings from which to execute his craftsmanship is also apparent from original sketches preserved.

Of active and studious disposition, it would seem that Robert allowed little or no time for amusement and was therefore thought ignorant upon the subject of sport. Nevertheless, as witnessed by his contemporaries, on occasion would be seen among the skaters upon the vast stretches of frozen flood water for which the Fens were noted, 'cutting the ice' as vigorously as in afterlife he was wont to tackle all his problems.

Whilst learning his trade with Rattee and Kett, save for Bury St. Edmunds, the young Robert seems not to have travelled far from the place of business, but upon the termination of his apprenticeship was soon on the move. By 1872 he had found himself employment as a journeyman with a craftsman of similar enterprise namely John Thompson of Peterborough, and while the work, consisting of sculpture and carving, ostensibly concerned the Cathedral of that city, where Thompson was engaged upon the constant task of restoration, it would seem that his job over the next few years took him to numerous other places.

In 1873 he was at Eye Church, Hereford on the repair of gargoyles; in 1874 at Rounds Church, Northants, carving capitals and a lion's head, and in 1875 engaged on the restoration, then in progress at Chester Cathedral - part of a letter addressed 'R. Bridgeman Carver, The Cathedral, Chester, postmarked 'Peterborough Nov 3. 75' is to hand; also a pencil sketch signed 'R. Bridgeman, 5 Parkgate Road, Chester.'

Back at Peterborough work on the Post Office Building (shields and diaper) is noted, and in an early time book for 1876 a trip to Lincolnshire is recorded, visiting Broughton and Moulton, and the time of 7 hours for 'drawing at the Cathedral' (presumably Lincoln).

At Halkin Church, Flint, woodwork was being executed for John Douglas of Chester (forerunner of the Architectural practice of Douglas and Minshull later established at that place) and the name McVeigh, one of R. B's early associates appears.

The year 1877 saw Mr. Bridgeman in Yorkshire at Bridlington Priory from whence in the year 1878, as a married man with three young children, the final move to Lichfield took place where he was given the responsible position of head-sculptor and carver on the restoration of the west front of the triple-spired Cathedral recently commenced for the Dean and chapter under their new consulting Architect, John Oldrid Scott.

Property known as the 'Stoneyard' was occupied by Thompson for the preparation of the masonry but it is understood that a small shed near the Minster Pool where later stood the School of Art (since demolished) was utilised by Mr. Bridgeman for the carving. "IT WAS WHILE SO EMPLOYED THAT HE CAME UNDER THE NOTICE OF DR. BICKERSTETH THEN DEAN OF LICHFIELD (who) WAS NOT SLOW TO RECOGNISE THE MASTER-HAND AND MASTER-MIND, AND SELECTED MR. BRIDGEMAN TO CARVE ONE OF THE CENTRAL FIGURES ... MR. BRIDGEMAN'S WORK WAS SO MUCH APPROVED THAT OF 114 FIGURES ON THE WEST FRONT NO LESS THAN 64 WERE CARVED BY HIM".

Harradine apprec. LICH. MERC 14.11.13

As time progressed many more came to be executed under his direction at Quonians Lane, the building of the Art School necessitating the move thither.

where Mr. Bridgeman's own little business that was to expand and become known throughout the land was commenced.

So far as ascertained, except for one small insert appearing in the second edition of Lomax's Red Book for the Queen's Jubilee year of 1887, no form of advertisement was deemed necessary throughout the lifetime of the founder, a feature emulated by his successors until forced between the wars to succumb to the pressure of the times.

As before stated R. Bridgeman had found little time for outside activity but as a respectable citizen regularly attended his place of worship and in the year 1900, as had been his namesake at Burwell was made Churchwarden of St. Mary's parish Church, Lichfield - neither had he sought public office but his generosity was well known and in 1907 it was proposed that he be made Sheriff of the City.

The invitation was accepted and Mr. Bridgeman immediately made known his intention of offering to the city a statue of the King (Ed. VII) which would be the first of its kind to be erected in the whole country since the accession of His Majesty in 1901. The Council were unanimous in their agreement, permission was obtained from H.M. Office of Works and the figure was duly executed and placed in the Museum Ground to be unveiled by the Earl of Dartmouth.

Meanwhile in departure from his usual role, on September 8, 1908 occupying a carriage with the Mayor, Mr. Bridgeman fulfilled his duty in leading the retinue at the annual beating of the 'County' bounds known as the Sheriff's Ride. The thanks of those who enjoyed his hospitality en-route were expressed by the Mayor who "ALLUDED IN APPROPRIATE TERMS TO THE MAGNIFICENT STATUE OF H.M. THE KING WHICH WAS TO BE UNVEILED ON SEPT. 30" while others paid tribute to his public spiritedness and to "HIS PROFESSIONAL ABILITY WHICH WAS ACKNOWLEDGED THROUGHOUT THE WHOLE COUNTRY".

Lich. Merc. 11.9.08

On his part the Sheriff said "HE WOULD ALWAYS LOOK BACK ON THAT DAY AS A RED LETTER DAY IN HIS LIFE" though it was felt by those nearest to him the highlight of his career was experienced on the day of the unveiling of his statue (Wed. 30 Sept.) a ceremony of which he was justly proud, and notwithstanding later achievements, always looked back upon with nostalgic satisfaction.

At a meeting in pursuance it was proposed by the Mayor and Senior Alderman:-

"THAT THE BEST THANKS OF THE COUNCIL, ON BEHALF OF THE CITIZENS OF LICHFIELD, BE AND ARE TENDERED TO ROBERT

BRIDGEMAN, ESQ., ... AND THAT THE BEFORE MENTIONED VOTE OF THANKS BE SIMILARLY ENGROSSED ON VELLUM AND FRAMED FOR PRESENTATION TO THE SHERIFF" ... the document bearing the full text was duly presented and is now in the possession of Mr. Bridgeman's grandson - Mr. C.W. Bridgeman.

Other gifts to the City included the sailor figure on the Museum building 1905, and upon relinquishing his office of Churchwarden in 1909 to the Vicar and Congregation of St. Mary's Church "A CHASTELY-CARVED ORGAN SCREEN".

Obit. Lich. Merc. 8.3.18

With some reluctance in the year Mr. Bridgeman agreed to the proposal that he be nominated a Councillor, and in November of that year was elected as a representative of the South Ward, an office he held for three years, when in the year 1913 he was returned unopposed, and, though a comparative new-comer to the Council, was unanimously chosen and made Mayor of the City on November 9 at the Guildhall.

For the ceremony Councillor Bridgeman "Re-introduced the scarlet gown which was the robe of office of the masters of the Ancient guild of Lichfield the forerunner of the corporation and which extended from 1378, Rich. II., to 1584 when Ed. VI. granted the city its charter of incorporation".

Ever reticent of public life, from which it was said he shrank, Mr. Bridgeman was rather surprised when asked in 1914 to continue as Mayor. Thus late in life was reached the apex of a career that hitherto had been inseparable from a business so absorbing that no time had been permitted or indeed sought for diversion, and only latterly, with the aid of his two sons, and daughter (Mrs. S. Harrison) acting as Mayoress, was he enabled to combine with his normal activity that of the well-being of the City of his adoption.

In habit he was a man of moderation, taking little by way of strong beverage, rarely known to smoke, never heard to swear - the word 'confound' being sufficient invective - in character he was just, generous to those in genuine need, but of stern disposition applying equal discipline to work people, family and self.

Only two occasions are recalled of his taking a holiday - at the turn of the century on Doctor's orders, a week in South Wales; and a little before the First World War with his elder son a visit to Belgium principally to view an exhibition of art. No remission from business and the enjoyment of little or no private life doubtless were the factors that in the end impaired his health giving to him the appearance of one much older than he actually attained. He died 1st March 1918 and was buried in St. Michael's Churchyard.

ROBERT BRIDGEMAN

1844/5	Born	BURWELL
1860	Commenced work Burrells Engine Works	THETFORD
1866	Apprenticed with Rattee & Kett, Sculptors	CAMBRIDGE
1868	Probably working	BURY ST.EDMUNDS
1872	Journeyman for John Thompson, Sculptor	PETERBOROUGH CATHEDRAL
1874	Probably Foreman for John Thompson, Sculptor	CHESTER CATHEDRAL
1876	Probably Foreman for John Thompson, Sculptor	BRIDLINGTON PRIORY
1878	Head Sculptor for John Thompson, Sculptor	LICHFIELD CATHEDRAL
1879	Employing own labour force at Stone Yard	LICHFIELD
1882	Fully established as R. BRIDGEMAN, Sculptor, at Quonians, LICHFIELD	

CONNECTIONS WITH CITY AND COUNCIL

1907	Made Sheriff of the City
1908	Presented King Edward VII Statue, Museum Grounds
1910	Elected to the local Council
1913	Made Mayor of the City
1914	Re-elected Mayor of the City (at this time employing 224 workers)
1918	Died (1st March) in his 73rd year - buried St. Michael's Churchyard
1921	Memorial placed in Burwell Church by his son, J.H. Bridgeman

❃

1878 - 1968

THE CATHEDRAL RESTORATION AND THE FOUNDER

T he Cathedral at Lichfield, never properly recovered from the damage caused when Cromwell's army besieged and occupied the Close, was, in the year 1876, the subject of an appeal issued by the Dean and Chapter to enable the undertaking of a long contemplated renovation of the West Front.

This had been mooted so early as 1856 upon the appointment of Mr George Gilbert, afterwards Sir Gilbert Scott as Master of the fabric. Dying in the year 1878 his London based practice with the vacant post of consulting architect devolved upon his son John Oldrid, whose restoration of the buttressed South Aisle is well known.

A paragraph in 'THE ANTIQUARY' for Jan-Jun 1880 denoted that "CONSIDERABLE PROGRESS IS BEING MADE"; for Jan-Jun 1882 that "THE TWO WESTERNMOST SPIRES ARE NOW THOROUGHLY RESTORED"...; and for Jul-Dec 1884 "THE RESTORATION OF THE NOBLE WEST FRONT OF LICHFIELD CATHEDRAL IS FAST PROGRESSING... THE ARCADE OF KINGS, WHICH FORMS A STRIKING FEATURE IN THE FRONT WILL SOON BE COMPLETED, THOSE OF PENDA, WULFERE, ETHELRID etc (eight others mentioned) BEING IN SITU, WHILE THOSE OF KING DAVID, WILLIAM I., AND II., HENRY I., II., AND III., AND EDWARD I., WILL SHORTLY LEAVE THE STUDIO OF MR. BRIDGMAN IN LICHFIELD".

Thus the name 'Bridgman' ('E' omitted) appears for the first time.

The restoration was in the hands of John Thompson, contractor of Peterborough, and it is understood that Robert Bridgeman, a native of Burwell, and trained by Messrs. Rattee and Kett of Cambridge, was employed in the capacity of head sculptor.

For Thompson he had worked on Peterborough and Chester Cathedrals, and came to Lichfield from Bridlington at the age of 32.

A time book commenced July 6 1878 intimates that Mr. Bridgeman was responsible for 'setting on' his own labour force, and by 1879 virtually running his own small concern, most of the work being sub-contracted to him; - and as the Chapter at Lichfield unlike that of many cathedrals, employed no resident masons, the potential was foreseen so that at the close of the restoration in 1884, he was available to take over the maintenance of the fabric, making it the nucleus of a business soon to expand and absorb his abounding energy.

CRCO

THE PREMISES

I nitially the work was executed at the Stone Yard, a quadrangle at the rear of Nos. 30/34 Dam Street, owned by the Dean and Chapter and used by Mr. Thompson, but in 1882 the opportunity to acquire property adjacent to Mr. Bridgeman's dwelling in Quonians Lane was not missed.

First removing the buildings at the rear of his house and his new property (no.2) an area approximately 60 x 30 feet was exposed, over one end of which timber trusses were erected on brick piers to carry a corrugated roof with sky-lighting to the northern aspect.

The covered portion became the studio where the figures were modelled in clay, and cast in plaster to be reproduced in stone, first being dressed to shape by the mason (a process known as pointing) before completion by the carver. All the models were carefully preserved and placed on racks, a practice that continued until many hundred replicas adorned the walls to gather the dust of ages, and astonish and enthral posterity. The studio was called the 'Band-room' because a military band used to have its practice room hereabouts and this name has lingered throughout its history.

In winter, heat was obtained from free-standing stoves known as 'devils', and lighting, until the advent of gas, consisted of oil flare-lamps, a warm, though somewhat dangerous, mode of illumination. Rough off-cuts of hardwood were laid to form the floor which in all shapes and sizes were to remain until recent times. In one corner, to facilitate the sharpening of tools, a blacksmith's forge was installed for which an existing flue was utilised in part still observable.

The problem was soon to be lack of space. More masons were needed, while repairs to woodwork at the Cathedral had necessitated the employment of carpenters who, with their benches, had been assigned a place in the new studio; also carvers in wood had been engaged, and office accommodation was required.

The office problem was relieved when Robert Bridgeman went to reside at 21 Dam Street. His house at the Quonians was then made available for administration; the main room becoming his private office, and the smaller room for his clerk. The existing stairways were replaced by a flight of stone steps and access made to No.2 to connect with another small office and store. The rooms above were used for drawing and estimated. To provide a place for the execution of figure carving in wood, those over No.2 were made into one. This exposed the original timber construction, probably three hundred years old - the most ancient part of the premises. The apartment was at first reached by a vertical ladder from the lane, but later an open stairway from the 'band-room' was erected and it became known as the 'The Gallery'.

Upon the garden site adjoining the stabling a shed was built to which the masons, still working at the stone yard, were transferred and the stables used for storage or made remunerative by letting.

As time progressed these better conditions were further improved by the acquisition of more land and property. This, on the northern side and parallel with the foregoing was, at the time of the sale (date unknown), held by the trustees of the late Mrs. Durant. Upon it stood a brick building where the carpenters were put. Above this Robert Bridgeman constructed a lofty room with a barrel roof as a shop for his woodcarvers, and it was made accessible by an ecclesiastically-designed spiral stone staircase. There was also cottage property (now No.4) and, probably included in the purchase, another stable and loft near the entrance to the new studio, then an open passage. Here was made a place for the models to be cast, and the loft above, reconstructed to cover the passage, made a room for more carvers who at this time were divided to follow either the Gothic or Classical tradition. By now the remainder of the area had been covered, so enclosing the whole space of 60 x 30 feet.

Piece by piece other premises were added, a sawmill to contain woodworking appliances, an upper story to be used as a joinery department. For these the boundary as it then existed, describing an irregular curve, was taken as the building line - hence the curious lay-out.

About the year 1905 an investment in still more property was made. Parallel and again adjacent to the northern side this consisted of two cottages surrounded by a large area of ground. The cottages, named Chadstowe Place, built in 1871, were altered to become the temporary residence of Robert Bridgeman's elder son, Joseph, while the garden curtailed, permitted further expansion by providing land that technically became the builders yard.

About the same time numerous experiments on the drawing board produced a plan whereby the masons were given more adequate accommodation. To the original of 24 x 24 feet, shedding approximately 50 x 20 feet was added, constructed with an open side to permit free passage of air - this conforming with regulations to reduce as far as possible danger to health from silicosis. A tank for boiling alabaster was installed, and the blacksmith's forge, once in the 'band-room', was at sometime removed to the position it occupies now. The design allowed for the erection of a setting-out room to be superimposed upon the original structure, the roof of which was supported on heavy oak beams similar to those in the 'band-room'. However, it seems that the idea was abandoned in favour of a small wooden foreman's office on the ground floor, and the eventual substitution of a large room and timber storage covering both old and new workshops.

By now, also, the stables were being put to a more practical use. A flat-topped dray, called the drug, for the transport of stone had been procured, to haul which horses were kept. These, described as medium-weight vanners, were obtained from George Beech, a farmer of Hilliards Cross, Fradley (Joseph Bridgeman's father-in-law) and grazed upon a field adjacent to the old windmill in Grange Lane. Successively they were driven and looked after by waggoners, Gill, Windsor and Case.

Back in the 'band-room' a further innovation was the erection on strong girders of an apartment intended as another workshop, but as access problems intervened opportunity was taken to vacate the existing drawing office and make use of this new and larger room. The former drawing office was adapted to house the archives.

In 1907 or 1908, Mr. Bridgeman's son attained the property on the opposite side of the lane. This included No.8 Dam Street, which was to become his permanent home, and the adjacent City House with its extensive garden. The rear portion of this garden was taken to increase the Bridgeman premises on the southern side, making possible a further right angular extension to the masons' shedding. This latest purchase enlarged the area to cover approximately an acre, and extended to the Parish Boundary of St. Mary, once the eastern limit of the city where the lane had terminated.

An association with the name 'Quonians' is found, which though of obscure origin is mentioned in ancient documents and is thought to derive from the ecclesiastical custom of well-blessing. A canticle sung on such occasions having the first line Quoniam tu solus sanctus is produced as evidence; and from a deed of 1283 it is assumed the lane led to 'Quoniamswell', though no trace of the well has been found.

At some time a more up-to-date heating system was devised consisting of large bore piping, etc. centralised from boilers located in the casting place, mill, and stonemasons. It is known that the apparatus was reconditioned and the event probably coincided with the renovation of Ashley Church, which in 1909 entailed replacing the existing radiators and hot water pipes.

Ultimately it became expedient to amalgamate the wood-carving trade, the Classical section being transferred from their quarters over the casting shop to merge with their Gothic colleagues who had become established in the new room above the masons' shedding. To their vacated quarters the drawing staff was once more removed. As to the Gallery, access had been gained by ascending an open stairway from the 'band-room', but this was achieved now by reducing the estimators' room to form a corridor with an opening cut at the end. The estimating room was then made into a photographic room, while alterations on the ground floor provided a better entrance and a small cubicle to which the estimator was transferred. (A sink was put into the new drawing office and a dark-room formed for the processing of negatives.) The wooden stairway was left to afford communication with the 'band-room', but a further project to construct an overhead passage from the new drawing office to the workshops beyond, for which a doorway was actually made, was abandoned in deference to objections raised by those using the thoroughfare below - this would certainly have become a 'Bridge of Sighs'.

So ended an epoch of pulling-down and building-up, leaving the premises in appearance much as they exist today.

CRBOD

MATERIALS, PLANT AND TOOLS

O n the masonry side all the English free, lime and grit stones, suitably chosen as to adaptability and environment, were worked.

For the Cathedral figures, a brownish-grey variety of sandstone from Penkridge had been used but for general work the local Staffordshire Hollington stone was to become much in evidence in the midland area. Foreign marbles and the English Purbeck from Dorset were also in use, together with alabaster, a material which for many centuries had constituted a pleasing medium for medieval sculpture and general craftsmanship, principally mural designs, effigies and work of monumental propensity. Obtained from the gypsum mines at Fauld near Uttoxeter and Chellaston in Derbyshire, its transparent nature sometimes needed to be deadened and, when highly polished, sealed. This was accomplished by boiling in a high-temperature immersion tank installed in the masons' department, or baking in a gas oven in the 'band-room'. In addition to Hollington, large blocks of stone obtained from many parts of the country were transported by railway and transferred on the drug to the yard, where it was neatly stacked to be sawn later into smaller blocks or slabs.

Varieties of limestone came from Hopton, Derbyshire; Portland, Dorset; Hornton, Oxfordshire; Clipsham, Rutland' and Doulting, Somerset. From Derbyshire the grit stones known as Stancliffe, Hall Dale, Darley Dale and Birchover were procured. On occasion a fine red sandstone was obtained from Runcorn, Cheshire; and for durability in extreme climatic or industrial environment a hard sandstone from the Forest of Dean, (a hard sandstone from Gloucestershire) was supplied. Yorkshire stone for paving, and varieties of slate from Cumberland and Westmorland for roofing and monumental work came into the yard. From Ireland and the Isle of Anglesey limestone was obtained, and from Scotland and Cornwall red and grey granite. This was mostly ready-worked because the hardness of the texture required special techniques and the use of pneumatic tools. For interior work a soft stone from Bath, Somerset and Caen, Normandy was used.

The stone was all neatly stacked later to be sawn into smaller blocks or slabs as required. Before mechanical aids were introduced the operation was performed with a cross-cut (a two handled saw), the sawyers being provided with a crude shelter in which to sit or stand one each side the block being sawn. For larger blocks a frame saw was used, the weight of which was counter-balanced by tackle suspended from a pole.

When the present mechanically operated saw (supplied as Patent No. 1553 John Smith 'Ketchley' Ltd.) was procured is unknown. Initially motivated by a vertical type steam engine, much hard labour was saved and economy effected as blocks and slabs of various thicknesses could be sawn in one operation. First the blocks had to be lifted by a small crane on to a heavy platform on flanged wheels known as the saw-table, and thence by a short rail track set at right-angles, to their position beneath the blades, the rhythm of which, akin to the tramping of feet, came to have a distinct association with the premises.

The apparatus was economical as it required only one man to control it. Nevertheless constant supervision was needed, involving the manipulation of water from 'ceiling' jets to obviate overheating, alternated with the feeding of the cuts using a long-handled shovel with an admixture of yellow sand and abrasive in the form of shot. It was a monotonous job; in all weathers, not sought but reluctantly accepted as the occasion demanded. Presumably too the engine would require some attention from time to time. The first crane was replaced by a larger one, the jib of which was of pine wrought from a single tree-trunk; and this in turn was superseded by the crane in use at present, also a Ketchley product, of latticed steel secured firmly by heavy girders set into concrete. Provided with gears it is said to be capable (though not expedient) of lifting a block 5 tons in weight.

Meanwhile, the expansion of the saw-mill with joinery accommodation over, observable as having evolved in three phases, made possible the installation of woodworking machinery. To save the burden of much handwork probably first on the list would have been a circular saw, which followed by other appliances would be the nucleus of the numerous mechanical aids later to be seen.

How the first machines were driven can only be surmised. Utilisation of the steam potential seemingly unlikely, the installation of an internal combustion engine placed at the position of the heating chamber may be considered an early acquisition. Such was a 'Bamford' product energised through the medium of diluted gas. To it all the machinery and eventually the stone saw was harnessed, the motive power being transmitted by belted pulleys from a system of under-ground and overhead shafting. The completed mill area when fully equipped contained most of the up-to-date labour and time saving inventions including:-

Circular, jig and band saws, planing, thicknessing, and smoothing machines. A spindle for use with revolving knives in hundreds of shapes to effect the working of moulded surfaces.

13

A sinker for execution of intricate tracery work.

A sander; a mortising machine; and latterly, a lathe for turned work (hitherto sublet to specialists elsewhere); and a machine for dovetailing.

The engine, enclosed in a glass windowed wooden 'house' just within the mill entrance, gave good service for many years. Set in motion every morning and carefully maintained by Jack Dakin, its vibrating 'chud-chud' was heard continuously throughout the working hours of the day. Only on rare occasions did it give trouble - once due to difficulty in starting when an unexpected backfire blew off half of Dakin's reddish eyebrows and beard - and another mysterious stoppage that was eventually traced to a boy's cap that had been sucked through the exhaust into the mechanism.

Any misgiving that may have been felt when modern methods were introduced were soon allayed when it was found that these did not detract from the artistry required of the craftsman who must still execute by hand the intricacies of his profession.

For the execution of the different trades a variety of individually owned tools was required. In the masons' department were seen hammers of iron, dummies of lead, mallets of wood - picks, spalls, wallers, mashers, scabblers, axes - punches, points, and pitchers for rough dressing and chisels for cutting, jumbers for boring, boasters and claw tools for surfacing; and drags, scrapers, cockscombs for smoothing, hand saws, grub saws, cross cuts; tools for squaring, scribing and levelling - all of which constituted the masons' kit, most being of iron, tempered and sharpened by the blacksmith.

The stone carver had also to provide for himself tools to meet all demands - some for soft stone, others for the harder varieties, alternating with those for marble or alabaster, and on rare occasions granite. Including chisels, gauges, fishtails, punches, rasps, rifflers, points, bull noses, claws, etc, those for stone cutting were again mostly of iron, while those for marble and alabaster were of finest steel. With stoneworking tools, described as mallet headed, the lead dummy was used; but for the marble variety, cup headed, a small lump hammer of malleable iron, was considered preferable. In addition, those who combined sculpture among their accomplishments had to procure tools for modelling in clay. Varieties made from steel or brass wire in the form of loops bound to wooden handles and others shaped in box-wood were respectively known as scoopers and spatulas.

Even more numerous were the tools required by the wood-carver. Arrayed on the bench around each of the craftsmen, these had to be seen to be believed, the old hands having in front of them as many as a hundred varieties from which to select at a glance the one most appropriate to the need of the moment.

Multifariously shaped gauges were prominent, interspersed with parting tools, fluters, veiners, fishtails and spadetools, all in fine steel set in wooden handles of ash or beech. Chisels ranging from 1/32 to 1 inch in width, and the corner firmer, an obliquely shaped chisel was useful among other purposes for the cutting of stencils and patterns. Even in those days, in advance of modern technology such tools were metrically catalogued and labelled as 1 to 25 millimetres.

There were also punches for frosting (a background feature of some of the styles) and, for identification, all the handles of the tools had the name or mark of the owner stamped upon them.

It was the owner's responsibility to keep his tools sharp, for which stones of carborundum and slips scooped and shaped by constant rubbing were to be seen, lubricating oil and hides for stropping and honing too. Lastly the carver's mallet made from the hard holly, beech or lignum vitae was used for 'knocking off the rough' and the finesse was accomplished by guiding and striking the tool with the palm of the hand.

Perhaps the snuff-box and water-bottle should be mentioned too for the wood-carver was usually a great snuff taker and water drinker, somewhat in contrast to certain in the stone trades whose taste was for stronger beverages; a habit carefully concealed from the management.

As in the mason's art much variety of material was required, so did the woodcraft demand all types of timber compatible with style, category and finish, though generally for ecclesiastical work oak was the basic medium.

In the early days logs - newly felled tree trunks - came into the yard to be stacked and dried, the maturing process sometimes taking twenty years.

A note in Lomax's Red Book for 23rd January 1914:-

"announced that Messrs. R. Bridgeman & Sons have secured the biggest oak in Herefordshire, reputed to be a thousand years old, its height when standing was 85 feet, and the girth 19 feet: when felled it weighed 30 tons".

Beyond the workshops, drying sheds were erected, and a pit was formed over which the logs were sawn into planks by hand, quartered or through and through as required.

The disposal problem of the sawdust inevitably created was somewhat offset by the requirements of shopkeepers in the butchery and kindred trades whose errand boys were seen on the premises, or the agent of an occasional travelling circus, with their sacks which they were permitted to fill for a few coppers.

When sawn, the planks were carefully segregated, those free from sap, uniform in colour and well figured, being chosen for the best contracts, while the knotty specimens, if otherwise sound, were used for rougher work.

The Victorian era had seen much ecclesiastical furniture made of pitch pine, a distinctly marked resinous wood emanating from the U.S.A. Occasionally the firm was required to follow this medium in the supply of additional fittings, but the Bridgeman role was more often to remove the existing and replenish with oak, hence the numerous relics seen from time to time on the premises. The pines and firs, under the heading deal, were the normal materials used for backing and grounds for fixing, while soft wood, mostly bay, was specified for the execution of sculptured figures and decorated work.

Leaving the sawyer, the wood was listed then brought to the machine shop to undergo the necessary processing before reaching the joiner whose job it was then to construct the article to be reproduced from drawings prepared by the draughtsman.

Here again the craftsman needed to be master of an almost limitless variety of tools:-

Saws: rip and cross cut, for cutting along and against the grain respectively, pad saws for keyholing; bow and fret saws for shaping, tenon, panel, bead, compass, and hack saws. For general bench work numerous chisels were required - firmers, bevel edged, swan necked, socket and mortisers. Trying, jack, smoothing, shoulder, and thumb planes. Rebaters, trenchers, routers for grooving and moulding. Braces used with countless bits for drilling. Awls, gimlets, and augers for boring. Hammers of different patterns - heavy and light. Screw drivers - large and small. The adze for chipping and smoothing. These with squares and templates, together with instruments for measuring, marking and testing comprised the miscellany of equipment to be found in the joiner's tool chest.

In addition, various appliances (often home made) were essential - bench hooks, shooting boards, mitre blocks, gadgets for trimming and the like. With the implementation of machine tools much hand sawing and planing was obviated, whilst trenching, grooving, and moulding could be expedited with accuracy. Boring and sinking became easy and, whilst this was to make some of the craftsman's choice tools obsolete, nevertheless to obtain the desired effect, reversion to old methods was demanded on occasions. The true flavour of the Jacobean style for example could best be achieved by using an adze, and the old hand would never dispose of his former outfit however unlikely the prospect of its return to favour.

Finally the accessories under the heading plant, effects and stock in trade necessary for the efficient running of the business should be mentioned. Unlike the artisans, those performing the menial tasks needed few or no tools of their own, but were expected to be conversant with the apparatus and tackle belonging to the establishment.

Heavy blocks of stone had to be handled and transported from place to place. For short distances removals in the workshop, metal rollers (iron tubes about 2 ft. long x 2" diam) were provided, but when taken elsewhere on the premises a hand truck of heavy construction was used for the blocks. This truck was called the bogie and consisted of a 4" block of hard wood mounted on two solid wooden wheels. An iron rod with a cross bar forming a 'T' handle was attached to the block, thus permitting the truck, when loaded, to be manipulated by two workmen.

In the builders' section of the yard there were poles of fir wood for scaffolding. These were reared at an angle to rest each side of a horizontal rail attached to a triangular frame. To give solidity when in use the poles were set in tubs weighted with earth or sand. Ladders of varying length, calculated in rungs, were hung on 'sky hooks' attached to the underside of the joists supporting the floor of the carvers' shop, now forming the ceiling of the old masons' shed. All was under the supervision of Ted the storeman, who jealously guarded and kept track of equipment going out or coming in. This including ropes and tackle, buckets and brooms, barrows, picks and shovels, belts, sawblades - not to mention the screws and nails, hinges, locks, bolts and much more which he meticulously recorded in his own department.

For the joiners a long line of wooden benches, standard as to pattern, fitted with a vice for holding the piece of material being planed or glued, were placed cross-wise down the centre of their shop. Each man was allotted a bench and so long as he remained in the firm's employ this became virtually his own, for communal use iron cramps were supplied, together with handscrews, dogs and holdfasts.

Up and down the country the carpenter's bench would be a familiar sight but in this instance less familiar would be the nature of the work for which they were utilised, also not so well known the addendum of the carver and mason.

Masonry consisting of the cutting and shaping of heavy blocks of material required that the 'work table' too be strong and safe to work upon. This was assured by the erection of a contraption made up of two stones supporting a thick slab of stone or slate known as the banker. Every man was given a 'work table' which, together with a little space round about became his place.

The stone carver and sculptor also needed a substantial support and for them a strong wooden stand (erroneously styled banker) was in use. On it the sculptor erected his armature - the skeleton upon which his models were built, consisting of a wrought iron bar (the spine) with bendable lead piping attached to position the arms and legs. The main bar would be firmly secured to a block of wood forming the base. At the head and other points, wood blocks were fixed and wires with butterflies (small cross pieces) to which when coated with shellac, the clay would adhere. Until cast a model required frequent damping - for this a garden syringe was employed and at night it was covered with a cloth previously well soaked.

Carving the figure created more of a problem, but this was solved in various ways - ropes, wedges and cement playing a part in making all safe.

For sculpture in wood the figure block was fixed with coach screws to a vertical plank several being reared permanently between the floor and ceiling of the gallery. On a bench nearby, the tools and accessories including callipers, dividers, enlarging compasses etc were arranged. Also in evidence were the pointing machines. The woodcarvers were provided with a continuous high bench reaching the full length of the two side walls of their shop with another of similar dimensions stretching down the centre of the room. On these were laid in super abundance the tools while the pieces being carved were secured with holdfasts fixed to pillars of metal passing through holes in the bench top. These had pivoted arms that could be raised or lowered with turn- screws. Here the foliage carving was produced - also courses of vine and oak; paterae depicting the rose and the thorn; panels of holly, thistle, honeysuckle, blackberry, seaweed, wheat; and elaborate tracery. The high finish and artistry of these works were made possible by the excellent tools and devices supplied to or owned by the craftsmen.

CR8O

THE WORK AND THE RECORDS

N ot only as a sculptor and carver of figures but in all branches of the architectural profession Robert Bridgeman was soon to manifest his skill and business acumen not only as a sculptor and carver of figures but in all branches of the architectural profession.

This may be gleaned from the carefully indexed and preserved records including all drawings, scale and full size, from the 1880s, models, patterns, and approximately 5,000 glass negatives of work executed, all indicative of rapid progress.

Primarily a constant flow of orders was received from the consulting architect, Mr. John Oldrid Scott (son of Sir Gilbert) for work on the fabric of the Cathedral:-

1886: Restoration of windows, Chapter House; 1887: Restoration of windows and buttresses to Lady Chapel; 1888: Repairs N.E. window and N. Doorway; 1889: N. Aisle, Nave and Transept; 1890: Vestibule' 1891: Cross to Central Gable; 1892: figures for Lady Chapel 'for the sum of £30 each'.

The year 1893 saw the restoration of the Central Spire. Extracts from the estimate dated February 22nd can be quoted:- 'working all new pinnacles and other stones as mentioned in Blackburn's estimate (including carving to crockets) and delivering at the Cathedral for him... restoration of large windows at foot of spire including all pinnacles, crockets and finials... 8 new pinnacles, 8 feet high on brochure of spire... as shown on architects drawing... Pilsbury estimate as appended for taking up the present lead gutters and relaying with new lead.

The estimate in four parts:- Blackburn, £290; Bridgeman, £234; Pilsbury, £30; extras, £6; totalled £470.[†]

Blackburn, presumably, was the steeplejack.

Much work for which academic craftsmanship was not required is also observed - orders for rough carpentry, clearance of gutters, pointing, cleaning and other accessories - these came directly from the Dean and Chapter to Robert Bridgeman, whose reply, prefixed 'Very Revd & Revd Sirs' invariably commenced 'I am willing to undertake'.

In addition to J.O. Scott other names appear - Baker, King, Chatwin, Moore, Paley, Austin, Tapper and, significantly, George Frederick Bodley, the designer

---

[†] *Cathedral account book.*

responsible for much of the artistic work at Hoar Cross Church. All were architects of distinction, with whom, and many others, the firm was to maintain a constant association.

Robert Bridgeman's versatility was recognised early by Arthur Baker for whom, in 1883, a lectern was made for Llanberis, N. Wales. This was followed by work at Llansiln, Abergele and St. Barnabas, Kensington. Of more local interest the drinking fountain on Greenhill was designed by Arthur Baker to be executed by Robert Bridgeman in 1886.

The scope, consisting of monumental masonry, from simple gravestones to intricate tracery and vaulting, side by side with examples of high quality joinery and specimens of carved woodwork in many styles, was soon to be observed, and the name known, throughout the country.

A widening field of operation is evidenced in that before the turn of the century major contracts, both ecclesiastical and secular, were being accepted, not least the gothic facade and elegant tracery-vaulted and carved interior of the John Ryland Library at the Dean's Gate, Manchester, including a series of portrait statues of eminent scholars in the field of literature, science, and arts, from Homer to Dalton, all under the direction of the architect Basil Champneys. This accounted for a lengthy period of activity, and was followed by a similar spell at Manchester Cathedral.

Elsewhere an abundance of work was in progress. These were important undertakings at Ambleside, Holyhead, Douglas in the I.o.M., Greenwich, Hertford, Slough, St. Asaph, Selby Abbey, Soutwell Cathedral, Mansfield College, Oxford, Newnham College, Cambridge, and, fore-runner of much work later despatched abroad, in Grahaemestown, South Africa.

Meanwhile, nearer home, following the tradition of Messrs. Farmer & Brindley, Sculptors of London, and under the guidance of G.F. Bodley and his partner Thomas Garner, the firm was employed in connection with alterations at Hoar Cross Church, in a contract which commenced in 1891 and intermittently continued until 1912. During this period many sculptured angels were executed (the edifice being named 'The Church of the Holy Angels').

The tomb of Hugo Francis Meynell Ingram to whose memory the church was dedicated in 1876 was executed in 1907, and a kneeling figure of Frederick Meynell was placed in a niche at the west end in 1911. The figure was modelled and carved by George Bindon and a note by Lawrence Weaver in his book Memorials and Monuments describing the benefactor as a man of marked personal piety, says:- "It was therefore appropriate that Mr. C.G. Hare should adopt a devotional motif for the memorial... and there was none more fitting than the representation of the deceased kneeling at a prie Dieu" while " the old difficulty of modern costume was well avoided by showing Mr. Meynell clad in court dress".

Mem. & Mon. Weaver.

The oak ceiling and rood to the Chancel were also the work of Bridgeman and subsequently tablets of recognition to both architect and sculptor, designed by C.G. Hare, Bodley's successor, were placed in the church.

Much 'running to and fro' was undertaken by railway, horse-drawn vehicle, and on foot, while transport of material, plant, and articles of furniture to the various sites was by goods, passenger train, or drug, according to distance or nature of load.

Letters were handwritten, and drawings despatched without wrappings, to be safely received at their destination, sometimes London, on day of posting.

Occasionally an old drawing comes to light with directions superscribed and postage attached.

All correspondence was duplicated in the manner of the time. Letters and estimates, written in copying ink, were impressed in a book containing leaves of tissue which had to be previously dampened with water using a flat brush. This was the job of the juniors as was the copying of drawings by hand traced on 'see through' paper.

The period of the South African War (1899-1902) seems not to have disrupted the general routine, nor, compared with later experience, was the aftermath materially affected by the memorial trade.

With one exception, the few executed consisted of utility articles or murals - for example the windows and regimental tablets placed in the Cathedral under the supervision of Walter Tapper. The exception was the monument erected in Duncombe Place, York. This, designed by G.F. Bodley, stood 57 feet high and was surmounted by an Edwardian cross. Octagonally shaped, the sides incorporated niches containing sculptured figures representing all branches of the services, below which were inset lettered slabs. These in Cumberland slate, contrasted with the remainder which was of Ketton stone and were inscribed with the names of those from Yorkshire whose lives had been lost. The memorial was unveiled by Field Marshall Earl Roberts, V.C. 3rd August 1905.

The sailor figure was thought inappropriate and was replaced by one unarmed. The original with projecting rifle was given to the local Council by Robert Bridgeman and placed on the Museum Building, Lichfield. Sometime damaged it now appears to be holding a sawn off shot-gun.

Subsequently the firm became engaged in other spheres. Following extensive alterations to the home of Mr Alfred Bird of 'Tudor Grange' Solihull in 1903 the involvement of all the interior fitting was entrusted to Mr. Bridgeman by the architects Messrs. Mansell & Mansell of Birmingham. The scheme included panelling, pilasters, overmantles, etc. in oak: ornate frieze mouldings and ceiling devises in fibrous plaster; and simultaneously, statuary; fountains, seats and other features in Portland stone provided for the newly laid-out grounds.

Mr. Bird, proprietor of 'Bird's Custard Powder', became M.P. for Wolverhampton and was made a baronet, but some years later Sir Alfred was accidentally killed while crossing the road near Westminster when the property, drastically altered, became a school for girls.

Similar contracts were carried out at Byrkley Lodge, Rangemore, Burton on Trent, for Lord Burton; at Kedleston Hall, Derbyshire, for Lord Curzon, including a carved recumbent figure in the private chapel; and at Swinfen Hall near Lichfield for Colonel Swinfen Broun, where the firm was engaged at the outbreak of the Great War in 1914.

Meanwhile, Mr. Bridgeman, a prospective member for the local Council in 1907 was made Sheriff of the City, when he conceived the idea of a memento in the form of a statue to be placed in the Museum Grounds.

The gift was to commemorate his year of office and that of the city's loyalty to the sovereign, King Edward VII, whose effigy in robes of state was to be the motif. A full size model was made from which the statue was carved, duly erected, and unveiled by the lord Lieutenant of the County on September 30, 1908.

As usual the plaster model was exhibited on a platform in the 'band-room' at the works, symbolically to survey his subjectry until figuratively dethroned in after years by others.

By this time Mr. Bridgeman's two sons Joseph Henry and Ernest Robert, who had acquired working experience and were helping with the management had been made partners and the firm became known (1908) as Robert Bridgeman & Sons.

Mr. Joseph continued to help his father, while Mr. Ernest (who incidentally had taken and processed many of the photo records) made alabaster a speciality, introducing and developing a side line afterwards to be absorbed in a business known as 'British Alabaster'.

For this a number of lathes were installed in the masons' department upon which were turned 'the bowls' (hanging light shades).

These in many shapes and sizes, often elaborately carved, were supplied through contacts in different parts of the country to domestic and commercial houses -

some provided for ocean going liners, the ill fated Titanic being named as one.

The carvers' shop, conveniently situated, became the polishing room, the carvers being returned to their old quarters, while the masons were temporarily crushed into the new right-angular wing of their workshop which they dubbed 'the tramp ward'.

The photo room was converted to an office from which Mr. Ernest and his secretary, Queenie, controlled the business.

A few years later to commemorate the mayoralty of Mr. Godfrey Benson, (afterwards Lord Charnwood) and the coronation of 1911 the order from the local council was received for the carving of the medallions of the king and queen (King George V and Queen Mary) that were added to the facade of the Guildhall which following the usual formalities were entrusted to sculptors G. Lowther and F. Thomas.

These were to create an amount of local interest but were but a small example of the vast amount of work at the time being executed and it could now be claimed that in addition to the ecclesiastical needs of the diocese and beyond numerous colleges and schools, various municipal, business and public institutions, inclusive of banks, hotels and hospitals, together with period houses, contained examples of the Bridgeman craft.

This in stone, marble, alabaster and wood could be found as far afield as Scotland at St. Cuthbert's Edinburgh, Cockermouth and Cartmel in the Lake District; St. Davids', Pembrokeshire; Norwich and King's Lynn, Norfolk; also at St. Albans', Canterbury, the London area, and the south.

In the Midlands, Birmingham and the Black Country the churches had been well served and the wants of the smaller towns and villages well supplied.

Outstandingly in Staffordshire under G.F. Bodley, a project lasting about three years had taken place - the complete restoration of Ashley Church, while again of local interest at the Cathedral for Mr. J. Oldrid Scott "The building of the present organ chamber in red sandstone with 'fireproof' ceiling had been executed".

The year 1914 saw the decease of Mr. Scott and the firm came into closer contact with Sir Charles Nicholson of London, it being announced "5th June... that Sir Charles Nicholson, F.R.I.B.A., has been appointed consulting architect at Lichfield Cathedral in succession to the late Mr. J. Oldrid Scott".

Sir Charles' expert methods of restoration were to ensure results at once practical and unobtrusive, and in addition to that on the Cathedral, his work was soon to be known throughout the diocese.

THE MEN

The first craftsmen recorded as working under John Thompson were Bridgeman, Smith, Wainwright and Reece. The work in hand for week ending July 6th, 1878, was finials and crockets' 3rd tier arcade, for which a corroborative note appears in Robert Bridgeman's cash book headed: 'drawn on account for carving to 3rd section S.W. Tower - first entry - 7 July 13 received... £10 0s 0d.' The debtor of the account is referred to as Mr. Thompson, the creditor Robert Bridgeman. Two weeks later (July 27) the name Knowlson appears on the list, followed by that of Hambling, Constantine, and Elliot.

During 1879: Charnock, Owen, Schofiled, Tayler, Whall, and McVeigh were mentioned; in 1880 Hewden, T. Allen, Pashley, Chambers and in 1881: Loveday, Hewlett, Boy, Maxwell*, Bull J.,* Bull W., Blurton*, Breman, Finn, Lowther, Roddie, Hollerton, Martin, and Bursill. (*Maxwell, J. Bull and Blurton were masons).

The apparently large number of employees in those days was not indicative of a growing staff, but characteristic of the time. Carving was a precarious occupation and many were forced to wander from place to place to find a living. Actually the weekly average over the years recorded was eleven, the highest number employed at one time (Oct/Nov 1881) sixteen, while in December of the same year only three are found on the books. Nevertheless, most were masters of their trade, and many would be well known to Robert Bridgeman before coming to Lichfield.

Among them William Pashley was acclaimed the greatest "WITH RBT. BRIDGEMAN WAS RESPONSIBLE FOR THE SEATED KINGS OF ENGLAND...WOULD NOT BE CALLED A SCULPTOR (BUT A FIGURE CARVER)...BECAUSE MONUMENTAL MASONS CALLED THEMSELVES SCULPTORS"; and, that he considered himself 'nulli secundus' probably accounted for the short duration of his stay at Lichfield.

Other characters were Tayler, a stout man of inebriate habits who, when out of work, is said to have tramped the country earning a bit playing a tin whistle; and Jack Owen, apparently an oldish man, carved the coats of arms appearing on the stonework of the Railway Arch in St. John Street erected in 1851, and who, in later years, was noted as one 'always owin'.

Conversely, July/August 1881 saw the 'setting on' of the brothers James and

William Bull, two local men who stayed in the firm's employment for life, a precedent followed in September by a young man, George Lowther by name, who remained with Robert Bridgeman (and sons) almost continuously until his death in 1929, a period of 48 years. Each became an expert in his profession, James and William following the trade of woodcarving and George Lowther a stone carver of merit, whose work included many artistically sculptured figures (including the statue of King Edward VII which was unveiled in 1908).

James Bull, it will have been noted, commenced his career as a mason and learned the art of pointing. This he afterwards put to good account in connection with the many figures in wood that were produced by the various sculptors.

To these names that were to become household can be added that of Walter Martin whose connection was only to be interrupted by two years on work of national importance, and severed by early death in 1919.

Coinciding with the restoration at Lichfield Cathedral, other orders were passed to Robert Bridgeman by John Thompson, including work outstanding at Bridlington and Chester, figures for Bangor, and carving in various parts of the country; Thompson's account when finally closed on 1st January 1885 showed a balance to Bridgeman's of £26 10s 3d.

Robert Bridgeman had also been engaged in the vicinity on contracts of his own and now, entirely independent, was constrained to increase his staff, not only by the addition of masons and carvers in wood and stone, but a full complement of workmen including carpenters, joiners, cabinet-makers, casters, stainers, polishers and labourers. Among them was a boy of fifteen who came as a probationer to obtain an insight into the craft of woodcarving. His grasp of the art, combined with a talent for drawing, soon convinced the master of his ability and he was accepted as an apprentice.

His indentures, now possessed by the compiler of these notes, are summarised herewith:-

> This agreement setteth forth that I Robert Bridgeman of the city and county of Lichfield agree with Mr. John Keyte relieving officer of the said city, to take his son William Eaden Keyte to teach him the art and craft of a stone carver for the term of five years and seven months, from the seventh day of May one thousand eight hundred and eighty seven to the nineteenth day of December one thousand eight hundred and ninety two...the said William Eaden Keyte then at the time of this agreement being fifteen years and five months old, and the said John Keyte agrees to pay to the said Robert Bridgeman the sum of twenty pounds...and the said Robert Bridgeman agrees to pay the said William Eaden Keyte four shillings per week for the

first year and seven months, five shillings per week for the second year, six shillings per week for the third year, eight shillings per week for the fourth year and ten shillings per week for the last year. The said <u>Robert Bridgeman</u> to pay in addition to the above sums, the travelling expenses to and from, and allow four shillings per week for lodging...at any job further than three miles away from the city of Lichfield...

The agreement signed by and in the presence of each other on the same day was dated 18th July 1887, a postage stamp value sixpence being affixed and superscribed with the three signatures.

Eaden (known in those days as 'Billy') chose stonecarving as his career in preference to wood, an occupation that he carried through until 1935 when, upon the untimely death of his associate exponent of the opposite craft, turned again to woodcarving which he successfully accomplished, together with modelling and stone, until the end of his working life in 1947, a record of sixty years' service.

His first tutor was J. Allen, a widely read man of integrity. Robert Bridgeman's son, Joseph, who was at the time learning the trade of masonry became Eadon's friend and on occasion shared with him the same lodgings when out working together as stonework often had to be executed in situ.

A list enumerating his travels has the following short preface:-

Edgbaston being my first job away from home from whence I proceeded to London (West Kensington, Palace Avenue Hotel) at which place I worked for exactly <u>six months</u>.

After having a spell in Lichfield I enjoyed <u>six months</u> in the city of dreams, Oxford (Mansfield College). Afterwards, having a time once more at home, I journeyed to Manchester for four years, a period crowded with eventful experiences...then a break, once more back again to the restoration of the Cathedral, Manchester viz., a new porch facing exchange station...

There follows a list of approximately seventy places covering a large part of England and Wales where undertakings were in progress. These, mostly in the early days of his long association with the firm, often entailed work on a scaffold in inclement conditions.

At Dean's Gate, Manchester, he was to meet some talented colleagues: - Harry Searle, his superior, great in his day as carver and administrator; Markley; Dockrell with whom he lodged; and Wilkins. At Cambridge, Charles Gower, a gifted craftsman who was noted for his clever likeness drawings and caricature sketches; at Bangor, Charles Best; at St. David's Cathedral, William Ball, overseer of the masons and at home George Bindon, a London trained sculptor who became No. 1 on the list of employees; Felix Coomans, a French artist famous for misquoting English colloquialisms; Wildey the German, drinking his morning beverage to 'der tag'; Tommy Allen a jolly little man; and Freddie Thomas an ex Art Master.

Joining these heavily moustached gentlemen came Alf Acott from Gloucester and Alfred Bermingham, two good exponents in the art of foliage carving and also must be added Jack Gilbert, the caster, his assistant Harry Gatchet, and Sammy Clarke the blacksmith.

Sometime contemporary were:- Edward Jacques in charge of the woodwork department; Alfred and Fred Hunt, joiners and relatives of Robert Bridgeman; Jimmy Hunt, head of the classical carving but no relation to the other two Hunts. Jack Dakin, potential engineer. Tonks and Hodges, mill-hands; George Wardle, Clerk; Harry Duell, Storekeeper; Bill Grenfell and his assistant Harold Bland, draughtsmen; Albert Wootton, junior estimator; Tom Yeomans, mason's foreman; Denton, Hughes and Holloway, sawyers; all helped to bring the name 'BRIDGEMAN' to prominence.

By the year 1900 the number of employees had risen to 113, by 1911 to 129 and in 1914 to a zenith of 224 with sculptors and carvers 40; masons 19; joiners 32; machinists 8; polishers 6; labourers 29; blacksmith 1; draughtsmen, staff and administration 9, plus 80 distributed on outside work at Manchester, Keddleston, Glossop, Comberford, Bilston, and around Birmingham.

Overlooking the band-room was the Gallery where the wood sculptors were kept busy.

Here worked Mr. Harry Saunders, a native of Walton-on-the-Hill, Surrey, who had joined the firm as a young man in 1895; Samuel Harrison, coming from Messrs. Spooner & Orton, fairground specialists, and soon to become Robert Bridgeman's son-in-law; Augustus Clarke fresh from the South African War, a finisher; and Jim Bull the pointer.

In the woodcarving shop Jim Bull's brother William had now reached the position of foreman, having among his colleagues Fred Tipper, Charles Lofthouse, Len Hawkins, Charles Marson, (remembered as one who rode a bicycle with conspicuously narrow handlebars) F. Williams, H. Dawson, C. Hibbert, P. Lowe, and numerous others including young Billy and Alfred Bull now following in their father's footsteps. This feature of sons, grandsons, brothers, nephews, inheriting the skill of their forbears was to manifest itself in most trades, particularly that of the mason; the Bakers, Clarkes, Greens; and notably the Hamlets, whose ancestry can be traced through five generations.

Before Bridgeman's day, John Hamlet, master mason and landlord of the 'Black Boy' Northampton, arrived from that place at the time of the contemplated restoration of the Cathedral.

This was in conformity with ancient custom when 'skilled masons moved from place to place to assist in building the magnificent sacred structures'.

Apart from the fabric, evidence of his monumental craft may be seen on work within the walls upon which his name is inscribed.

He was also responsible for the erection of the Clock Tower upon its original site facing Bore Street in 1863, and for many years a business at 19 Church Street was run by his son Richard Henry and grandson Albert, the latter from time to time working for Mr. Bridgeman - his signature was observed among those written upon a scroll placed in the ball of the central spire at the time of the restoration of 1893 and recovered in 1949.

Eventually his two brothers Ernest and Arthur found employment at the Quonians, where apart from war years, they remained for life, and to anticipate, Ernest's sons, Richard and Jack were to follow, and Jack's sons again, Richard and Philip, when four of the name were to be seen working together under the same roof.

Prior to 1914 can also be named Amos Aust, Brockhurst, Roome, Ted Smith, Jimmy Clarke son of Sammy the blacksmith, and Walter Martin's son, Wally, who as young men became the original turners of the bowls.

About the year 1911, Mr. J.H. Bridgeman's son, Robert, came into the business to learn the art of carving, and a young man, Dutton, who had been a senior student at the Walsall School of Art.

Popular with the men, Mr. Bob soon became involved with their activities and instigated the formation of a cricket team that for a number of years practised in the nets and played matches on a nearby meadow called the Mill Croft. Their opponents consisted of local teams in and around the city - Kings Bromley, Chorley, Yoxall, Longdon, Rangemore, Wall, Alrewas, Walton-on-Trent and Lichfield 2nd being regular fixtures.

A typical team playing in 1914 as shown on the picture (*see centre pages*) are from left to right:-

Back row: Tom Ashcroft, Harry Dutton, Charles Martin, Jimmy Mapson, Alf Bermingham, Charles Hibbert, Alf Acott, Bob Brinham and Jack Draycott (scorer).

Middle row: Fred Williams, Fred Tipper (capt.), Robert 'Bob' Bridgeman grandson of the founder (vice capt.), H. Dillistone.

Front row: Percy Saxton and Alf Bull (for long the only surviving member).

Of these Tom Ashcroft was then masons' foreman - a steady bat; James Mapson, cabinet maker and french polisher - good fielder; and Bob Brimham, labourer and an ex-army fast bowler, also fast of temper, a dispute needing to be dealt with discreetly by the umpire.

Conditions of work and pay were very different from those of today. A normal working day starting at 7 a.m. (sometimes 6 a.m.) and finishing at 5.30 p.m. with breaks for breakfast and dinner was nine hours. Saturday working 7 to noon. The basic hourly rate of pay for a labourer was 5d: approximately 20 shillings per week. Masons and joiners received 7½d to 8d: 30 shillings. Sculptors and carvers averaged 10d (No. 12, Keyte W.E., week ending June 4th 1914, received £1.19.6d) no deductions, no tax, no holiday pay - no strikes. On the credit side living costs were low and static, as were wages - when you were in work.

Every Saturday at 12 noon the men filed past the entrance to the old stores where, through a small hatch in in the doorway, each received his salary, including golden sovereigns neatly wrapped in paper.

In those days the mid-day egress was one of the local sights. The Lane was filled to capacity by the workmen eager to make the most of their break. Their return was more leisurely, the men gathering in groups talking or quietly smoking until the 'bewitching' hour. Those on the fringe sat or squatted around - Mr. James Bull always first on the scene, claimed as his seat a stump (still in existence) placed at the corner of No.8 Dam Street to protect the brickwork from the hubs of vehicles. Jim was a quiet inoffensive man, adept at checking an argument with a shrug and his favourite expression 'some taken one way, some another'. Should no pointing be required, tracery cutting at which he was expert, would lead him to the carvers' shop.

The high standard of workmanship and versatility expected and given by the craftsmen had proved sufficient means of attracting the enquiries and orders of architects, laymen and clerics, no other form of advertising being necessary.

This was peaceful England but unfortunately to be disrupted, war clouds were gathering and soon the young men, including Mr. Bob, followed by the not so young responding to the call, were seen leaving their bankers, their benches, lathes and tools marching away to the strains of Tipperary.

Mr. Bridgeman, who had attained the highest civic honour as Mayor of the City, had now to use his energy in other directions, notably connected with his decision to issue an appeal to the citizens for monies 'To be transmitted to the Prince of Wales' National Relief Fund', and on September 18th (the 205th anniversary of the birth of Dr. Johnson, the day upon which he placed the usual laurel wreath on the statue in the market), it was announced that the fund had raised £1,464.4s.8d; and on the 9th of November at the annual meeting of the City Council, Robert Bridgeman was re-elected Mayor.

Among ecclesiastical contracts in hand at the outbreak of hostilities was woodwork for a church at Woolwich; alabaster work· at Acocks Green; and extensive fitments for the Guildford School Chapel at Perth, Western Australia, for Mr. Walter Tapper, St. John's Wood, London.

A part of the business that prospered throughout the war was the alabaster trade, and in this department, to 'Keep the Home Fires Burning' (their favourite song) a quota of female labour was employed.

As was to be expected, orders from the local depot at Whittington Barracks were received - notice boards, letter racks, items of furniture for the Officers' Mess etc., and a continuation of the project commenced in 1912 to completely furnish the Sanctuary of the Garrison Church together, inevitably, with memorials to the fallen.

The firm too was not to be without its losses; of the forty or so who served, Charles Carthy a reservist was killed in 1914, whilst Charles Turner (son of Billy, popular carpenter) headed the list of the local Territorials who lost their lives. Jack Adams, a young carpenter who had joined the newly formed Birmingham Battalion of the Royal Warwickshire Regiment was killed in 1916, and in the same year came the sad news of the death of Mr. Bob Bridgeman holding the rank of Sergeant, Royal Engineers, killed on the Somme on 5th November. Later news of the deaths of Harry Dawson and Fred Williams was received; also C. Martin and several masons including J. Macpherson who fell victim to the first influenza epidemic, and finally Bob Brimham, recalled and afterwards posted missing.

Others who went and returned safely (though not to their employment at the works) were Tom Smith, junior clerk; Alan Poynton and James Wood, junior draughtsmen; also Charlie Brown, too young for military service but who joined the drawing staff at Branston Machine Gun Factory.

By the end of the year 1914 the amount transmitted to the national fund is recorded as £1,626.13s.3d., and in the following year Robert Bridgeman, having completed his second term of office, relinquished his position of Mayor.

Meanwhile, his sons were becoming more and more responsible for the administration of the business and soon, due to his increasing ill-health, taking complete control.

Robert Bridgeman died 1st March 1918 in his 73rd year, his name having become famous in the sphere of his activity, not only throughout England, but also a much wider area where his work was to be seen (and still is) in places so far away as Adelaide and Perth, Australia; Grahaemstown, Bloemfontein and Fouriesberg, South Africa; Orebo, Sweden; and Hobart, Tasmania.

The funeral service at St. Mary's Church, attended by his employees and a large congregation, in the absence through illness of the vicar, Rev. Bolton was conducted by his principal curate, the Rev. H.S. Cresswell joined by the Rev. Cohle former curate and the Dean of Lichfield H.B. Savage.

CR&O

BETWEEN THE WARS

F ollowing the signing of the Armistice in November 1918 and subsequent demobilisation, the trek began of those returning to the 'Land for Heroes'.

The year 1919, week ending January 4th, had on the books a total of sixty-six men (and women):- sculptors and carvers 9, masons 10, joiners 8, machinists 6, labourers 6, Turners 10, polishers 7, blacksmith 1, draughtsmen and staff 5; outside work 4.

Soon these were to be augmented by the 'demobbed' - to the band-room came Acott, Batkin, Bermingham, Dutton, Vinell, and Walter Martin, all of whom had served in the forces or done work of importance elsewhere.

H. Saunders and 'Gus Clarke returned to the gallery: and to the woodcarvers came back Haycock, Hawkins, Marson, Wright, Billy and Alf Bull. (Alf as a young officer having taken part in the crossing of the St. Quentin Canal).

C. Marson, hailing from Kings Bromley, was a meticulous tracery cutter. During the war his instinct for precision led him to the air industry to become expert at propellor shaping. Remembered are his corpulent figure, never varied attire, stiff white collar, well polished ox-blood shoes, large cloth cap, and of course his 'bike', hitherto noted for its unique handlebars. Trevor Wright, an athletic type, later emigrated to South Africa to join the Rhodesian Police Force. To the joinery department, following work of national importance, Harry Phoenix who had joined the firm in 1895 was reinstated; also James Maunder (1912); and Jim Linforth (1913) returned to their benches; while from the forces came J. Mapson, who had served in the Royal Engineers; P. Harvey, J. Evans, and J. Dakin, (Junr.). Among those who had remained the names Turner, L. Davis and H. Evans had become household; while others not to be forgotten were Fred Ollivier, native of Guernsey, Lewis Dawson from Armitage and George Boggis (relative of Mr. J.H.B.) from Thetford - the two latter as new men to become established members and remain at Bridgeman's for many years.

Over all was Charles Pennington who had taken the place of Edward Jacques as foreman. C.P. was a fine craftsman, administrator and gentleman, and had been with the firm since 1898.

To those below in the sawmill (Tonks, Capper, J. Dakin, (Senr.), and J. Brown), was added Walter Martin's nephew Ted who had commenced his career as a

32

handyman in 1912, but after the war became an expert mill hand, stainer and polisher.

Walter's stay, upon his return, lasted but a few months when overtaken by the illness that was to precipitate his death, but in other spheres the name Martin was made inseparable from that of Bridgeman when Ted's elder brother joined the establishment to become 'Jack of all trades' and to be seen on the premises over a period of 45 years.

A baker by trade but well able to adapt himself to his new environment, Jack became a most useful addition to those working 'back stage'. Taking the place of old Jack Wright who for many years had stoked the fires, kept the shops tidy, cultivated the waste ground at the rear, all these jobs and more J. Martin vigorously tackled.

Entrusted with the keys, virtually day and night, weekday and Sunday, Jack kept a watchful eye on the property. Always willing to perform the dirty jobs one remembers his oft-time dishevelment at the end of the day going home proverbially 'as black as the grate' but always to appear the following morning 'spik and span' in clean shirt and brilliantly polished boots which he had 'boned' - a process learned in the army. On rare occasions he would be absent due to an emergency, his former employer having appealed for his help at the bakery.

To become his colleagues were Harry Hatchett just returned from war work at Branston Factory, and Mrs Starkey engaged as a cleaner during the crisis. Classed as a labourer but with more than average ability, Harry, among other talents, perfected the art of casting, the rudiments of which he had acquired from his predecessor J. Gilbert, also expert at cleaning stone and marble, periodically he was sent to Edinburgh where in 1906 at St. Cuthbert's Church a mammoth 'Last Supper Relievo' had been executed and placed around the apse of the Sanctuary. With the order a five yearly visit for its upkeep was stipulated and Harry's pilgrimages thither led to him being ever after alluded to by his colleagues as 'MacHatchett'. For many years the plaster model was to be seen among the casts adorning the walls of the band-room.

In charge of the stone and alabaster trade was Tom Ashcroft, who had succeeded T. Yeomans and occupied an office midway between the masons and turners. Under Tom a number had remained throughout the war including the Baker brothers George and Bill, T. Glithero, F. Wootton, and E. Hamlet, while to the vacant bankers and lathes now came back Jimmy Clarke with tales of adventure on the Western Front; E. Hamlet's brother Arthur from service in Mesopotamia; S. and J. Avery, B. Baker; and others new to the firm - Hardy, Searcy, Willer, etc. Teddy Price from Clungford, Shropshire (residing at No.4 the Quonians) was the blacksmith and the labouring force can be named as:- Allport, Courrie, Davis, Emery and Mytton.

The office staff consisted of Harold Bland, long installed as senior draughtsman; E. Fisher and W. Wootton, estimator and cashier; J. Hall, junior clerk; and Ted Waltho, storeman and timekeeper. Coming to Bridgeman's in 1906 with experience as a school porter and asylum attendant Ted had made himself an institution, and though of stormy disposition his keen sense of humour had ensured popularity with all except perhaps the defaulter arriving late who found the rack containing his ticket removed meaning the loss of a quarter hour of his pay - to remonstrate would have invoked a tirade.

The telephone had been installed in 1897 for which a cubicle was formed below the stone stairs. To call the exchange (41 Wade St.) a handle attached to the instrument had to be vigorously turned and with a small 'cup' to your ear you shouted into a funnel shaped mouthpiece giving the name and number required. R. Bridgeman (Lich. 34) was among the first fifty subscribers.

Also a telephone system, energised by wet batteries, existed between office and works; a typewriter, competing with Ted Fisher's meticulous copper-plate hand writing had been procured; and a heavy frame for sun-printing - a fair weather occupation by which under ideal conditions a clear copy of your drawing could be obtained. To develop, only water was required - very economical!

Sometimes the drawings were photographed by Mr. Joseph's daughter Margaret who, after a short period away, returned to her useful work. Miss Bridgeman was also proficient in the realm of decorative art, much in demand at the time, and worked on occasion side by side with professional artists. Sent by the architects to execute special orders, the names Jackson and Harper were familiar; and in 1919 Mr. Gray, who on the instructions of C.E. Bateman, Esq., responsible for the new alabaster reredos in St. Mary's Church, in the Market, literally covered it (and himself) with gold and colour.

Early in the year Samuel Harrison who had remained on the gallery throughout the war, left to join the firm of Jones and Willis, Birmingham, before establishing himself at his home in Lichfield, where he worked until his death in 1941. He took with him his son Ted who had recently commenced as junior to the wood carvers. Working for Bridgeman's at the time as journeyman mason was Fred Perry to whom Mr. Harrison let a part of his property on the Birmingham Road. Here Mr. Perry, later well known in the city as Councillor and Alderman, commenced his own small monumental business.

Mr. Ernest Bridgeman too decided to remove his part of the business to Weston, near Stafford, where for many years the concern functioned in work of an ornamental character - principally alabaster. This took from the premises a percentage of the tradesmen, including Alfred Bermingham and Harry Vinell, carvers; Wally Martin, Brockhurst and Rooms, turners; and eventually (1923) Harold Bland who later took charge of the business which became known as "The British Alabaster Bowl Co.".

The lathes worked by an underground shaft from a flywheel connected to the gas engine, were dismantled, and the female staff being made redundant, the masons and woodcarvers were now brought back to their respective quarters. The masons' bankers, returned to their original positions, were occupied in the following order:- Vic Green, Bill Baker, Amos Aust, George Hiden, Fred Wootton, Albert Truelock, George Green, Tom Glithero, Matt Wright, Ernest Hamlet, Jimmy Clarke and Tom Yeomans, the right angular extension beyond being used more comfortably by the remainder. Of those who had worked on the bowls, it will be noted that Aust and Clarke remained with the firm, while Ted Smith, previously mentioned, chose an army career, becoming a drummer in the North Staffords and serving for 21 years. Mr. Ernest's vacated office was used as a photo record room and library where valuable and interesting books relevant to the business were kept.

Among those left in the band-room were Bindon in advancing years and George Lowther, the latter a man of high principle combined with a sense of dry humour and subtle wit. An incident he loved to relate concerned his fine craftsmanship when, during the execution of an intricately carved feature on a small country church, a passing yokel having watched for some time remarked - 'Very good mister but I can beat ye at plowin'.

War memorials now became priority. Between the years 1919 and 1922, no less than one hundred and fifty-eight interior designs, often elaborately carved, were executed in stone, alabaster, wood and metal; approximately eighty wayside crosses, obelisks and varieties inclusive of the city's memorial in Guiting stone overlooking the Minster Pool, and a similar concept at Wednesbury both the designs of Mr. C.E. Bateman.

Also two colossal monuments designed by Mr. Bland were erected at the entrance to the Parade Ground at Whittington Barracks. These in portland stone were surmounted by the Egyptian sphinx and China Dragon in bronze, the insignia of the South and North Staffordshire Regiments respectively.

The masons, filling their quarters to capacity were found overflow accommodation in the band-room where Arthur Hamlet and other letter cutters coped with the continuous long lists of names.

During the year 1919 E. Fisher and W. Wootton obtained employment elsewhere, and in January 1920 Ashcroft left the firm his place being taken by Bill Chatterton a Londoner; but notwithstanding removals the number of work people had now risen to 99, by March to 104, and to a further peak in 1921 of 119.

To keep up with the influx of orders, numerous 'birds of passage' can be cited: Mr. Dawes, for a short time Mr. J.H. Bridgeman's secretary; Miss Turrel, typist; Reginald Earl, clerk, Mr. Vickers and Norris MacKay assistant draughtsmen; F. Revell, junior; and notably Mr. Hugh Burt from South Africa, a clever exponent of the classical style of architecture from whom Mr. Bridgeman's younger son, Charles, about to commence his career in the business received his initial instruction in the art of carving. During his stay Mr. Burt designed and executed two memorial plaques constituting orders obtained by him and despatched to Cape Town and Bloemfontein. Inadvertently the labels on the packing cases were transposed causing some consternation.

In addition to the memorial trade orders were being received in rapid succession from all directions. During the same period (1919-1922) church work alone accounted for thirty-nine concepts involving Sanctuary and Chancel fittings, twenty-five screens, three organ cases, numerous pulpits and fonts; various seating schemes and many small items in wood and stone. Also much exterior work including eight lychgates, and on the monumental side, approximately one hundred and sixty private grave memorials were executed.

In addition to those designed and provided exclusively for the clergy and laity many orders were received through the well known architects and their successors:- Messrs. Austin & Paley, Lancaster: Hicks & Charlwood, Newcastle on Tyne; William & Segar Owen, Warrington; Messrs. Connon & Chorley, Leeds; Healey & Healey, Bradford; Douglas & Minsull, Chester; Messrs. Heazell & Sons, Nottingham; Naylor & Sale, Derby; Powles & King, Nantwich.

Mr. A. Linton Iredale, a successor to Lloyd Oswell, Shrewsbury; W.H. Bidlake, Principal, Birmingham School of Architecture; Philip B. Chatwin, following his father, J.A. Chatwin. Mr. J.A. Swan, formerly Beck & Swan, Wolverhampton; Major Hubert Adderley (afterwards Lord Norton) of Fillongley, collaborating with W.H.R. Blacking, Christopher and Geoffrey Webb and others; among whom Louis Ambler, featuring high class monumental work of the Georgian period.

J. Arnold Crush, Harborne, with schemes for Catholic Churches; Messrs. Quick & Lee, Leamington, for whom the Clock Tower in the Jefferson Gardens at that place were erected and for which a scale model in wood was offered before procedure; H.J. Jackson, Coventry responsible for a new Church at Earlsdon. Mr. W.D Caroe, extensive fittings at Eccleshall; H.C. King long term contracts at

Brierley Hill and elsewhere; Sir Charles Nicholson, Cathedral restorations and much other useful work.

The three latter were London based as also Mr. C.G. Hare who had become partner to G.F. Bodley, and after his death, principal of the practice of Bodley & Hare, Grays Inn Square; and last but by no means least, Mr. Walter Tapper, once Bodley's senior assistant who had built up an extensive connection in the City and provinces from his office at 10 Melina Place, St. John's Wood.

Many of the forenamed at some time came to the premises to discuss new projects or inspect work in progress. Outstandingly the visits of Mr. C.G. Hare come to mind and those of the already mentioned, C.E. Bateman.

In rough tweeds (trousers tucked into socks) Charles Bateman often made the journey from his residence at Sutton Coldfield to Lichfield on a bicycle. His bushy eyebrows and half-lens pince-nez through which he would peer, genially or otherwise, are well remembered, as also his high pitched somewhat plaintive voice. A bachelor and keen angler normally so impervious was he of his appearance, that to fall into a bag of cement, it was said, would not in the least perturb him. His business in Colmore Row, Birmingham, inherited from his grandfather, was eventually to pass to his partners, Messrs. Hale, Goldsbrough, Blennerhasset, and Mr. E.M. Marriner, who eventually took control.

By contrast, the aroma of expensive Egyptian cigarettes, surrounding his sartorially correct attire is associated with the visits of Mr. Cecil George Hare. Aesthetically supporting himself on his bamboo walking stick containing a 5ft measuring rod released by a sliding silver cover C.G.H. (also a bachelor) was at once an impressionist and man of taste, the latter initiated through the media of his assistants A.V. Heal and R.V. Smith who produced many designs of merit.

Following the tradition of their predecessor G.F. Bodley, the gothic form of architecture was adhered to but with mouldings freely rendered and carved motifs unique in character adapted from seaweed patterns.

Sometimes the architect would be accompanied by his client and from time to time many distinguished clerics and celebrated laymen visited the premises. Of the former those connected with the Cathedral made frequent calls while among the latter can be cited Lord Curzon of Keddleston, the Earl and Lady Harrowby of Sandon, and, in 1919, one who had been much in the news during the war, the Admiral of the Fleet Lord Fisher for whom a memorial tablet in white marble was being executed to the memory of his wife for erection at Kilverstone.

By now (1919) the cricket team had been re-commenced, playing at home on the same pitch, and away against their former rivals. The team consisted mostly of new-comers supplemented by some of the old members, among them A. Bull and H. Dutton, the latter about to emigrate to Australia.

Those new included Mr. Dawes, A. Meir, F. Revell, a plumber named Grant, Mr. E.R. Standley who in 1920 joined the office staff in place of W. Wootton, Mr. Charlie Bridgeman, and a few friends not employed by the firm but who helped to keep the team going for several successful seasons. A keen supporter was Eaden Keyte, an enthusiastic follower and critic of the fine points of the game.

The formation of a football team, mooted at various times, seems not to have materialised, but there is an interesting connection. In 1920 the pony and trap that had been Mr. Bridgeman's means of conveyance, was replaced by a small car and driver by name Noel George. Serving in Salonica during the war George had played for the British Army, and upon his return signed on as goal-keeper in part time professional capacity at Wolverhampton. This evoked much interest among the men, particularly in 1921 when the 'Wolves' won through to the final of the English Cup, but unfortunately the match, one of the last to be played on the Crystal Palace Ground before transference to Wembley was lost, the opposing team, Tottenham, snatching a last minute victory, one goal to nil, on a water-logged pitch.

By this time not only Polly the pony but the remaining dray horse and his driver Harry Case had been replaced and a three ton Ford lorry was procured to be driven by Fred Button who was with the firm for many years, later becoming Mr. J.H. Bridgeman's chauffeur. Another who came during this period but not destined to remain long, was Joseph Drew, an art student from West Bromwich. After making good progress as a sculptor 'Jerry' as he preferred to be called, followed those who had strayed to Weston, but later settled at Ipswich where at 78 years of age (1975) he still pursues his craft. While at Lichfield he carved the lions 'sejant' in Guiting stone added to the brick piers at the entrance to the City war memorial.

Mr. J.H. Bridgeman was now in sole charge and, during the war, having become a member of the local Council, was in 1922 elected Mayor of the City, an office he held, as had his father, for two years.

In that year electricity was installed on the premises, taking the place of the old partly incandescent mostly naked-flame gas lighting. This was a private enterprise powered from batteries charged by a dynamo motivated in the engine house, a progressive step anteceding the town's conversion. Proving not too satisfactory it was eventually replaced by the City's own supply (ceremonially switched on on 14th July 1926) and, following modifications to the circuit, all the machinery including the stone-saw became energised from the mains and the engine and engine house just within the sawmill entrance were finally removed.

Early in the 1920s the idea of a distinguishing mark was mooted when a 'man' standing upon a 'bridge' overlooking a flowing stream was envisaged (a subtle play on the name and the passage of time) but this was shelved to be later improved by Mr. Charles Bridgeman at whose instigation a working bee became the firm's identifiable motif - the initial letter of Bridgeman combined with that of business.

Between the years 1923 and 1926 some big undertakings were carried through, notably at Wick, Pershore, in Worcestershire consisting of the reconstruction of a Victorian house called 'The Manor' to the Elizabethan style of architecture. This was under the direction of Mr. Cecil Hare and to produced the desired effect the materials were all carefully selected and approved by him - old timber and tiles from demolished buildings were procured, V shaped gutterings of teak supported by wrot'iron brackets used, and the plaster interstices relieved at intervals with motif panels. The main structure surrounded a cobbled courtyard, and at one corner a small chapel enshrining as its main feature an Altar Tomb upon which reposed a recumbent figure with dog at feet was erected. The effigy in Staffordshire alabaster, executed by George Bindon was placed in memory of the son (killed in the war) of the Reverend Bickerton Hudson for whom the residence was rebuilt. During the process Bindon became riled in that the dog, the work of another, evoked the more interest. Within the period of execution 18 men were permanently engaged on the site supervised by J. Edgar Walker, a man rarely seen at the Quonians, being engaged in similar capacity on outside contracts throughout the country.

Mr. J.H. Bridgeman, a keen preservationist, taking his cue from this masterpiece concurrently restored some property owned by him in Dam Street which afterwards became a popular cafe know as 'The Elizabethan'. Also he built a small house conforming to the same style, as a wedding dowry for his younger daughter and in which Mrs. Meacham as she became still lives (1975) in the lane known as 'Cross in Hand'.

From Wick, J.E. Walker went to Southsea, near Wrexham, where the church due to subsidence, had virtually to be rebuilt using a labour force of approximately 30, mostly local workmen predominantly of the name Hughes, Jones and Owen. This again was under the direction of Messrs. Bodley & Hare, as were Michaelchurch Court, Hereford; and much ecclesiastical work over a wide area including Strelley, Notts; Little Ness, Salop; Shrewsbury; Eastbourne; Middlesbrough; Forsbrook; and nearer home extensive fittings at St. Pauls Church, Walsall.

In line with post war improvements, commencing 1921, the London Joint City and Midland Bank (which then became, "The Midland") had many of their premises re-built or renovated, and the firm received orders for carving in Darley Dale stone at approximately thirty-five branches in all parts of the country inclusive of the refacing of their branch in Market Street, Lichfield. These, under the direction of Messrs. Gotch & Saunders, Architects, Kettering, mostly entailed cartouches, pediments and corbels executed in situ by H. Batkin and E. Keyte. All new premises had the name 'MIDLAND BANK' carved on the stonework, but when reconstructed, letters of oak were attached to the building. Many sets of these were executed at the works with face and sides overlaid with best English gold leaf or alternatively dull black paint. Also the interior fittings at Lloyds Bank, Lichfield, all in polished mahogany were executed about this time.

The year 1926 was notable as the only occasion when the management experienced a short period of 'labour trouble' brought about by the industrial crisis. The men were forced by their Unions to lay down tools as a sympathetic gesture in line with others who had been overtaken by the national strike in May of that year. Ironically this immediately followed a grand dinner given to the workpeople by Mr. J.H. Bridgeman on the occasion of the marriage of his two daughters, when speeches expressive of loyalty had been made on both sides.

In 1927, W. Chatterton, who had been with the firm for eight years returned to London his place being taken by Bert Portlock of Cheltenham who had worked for both Martins, and Boltons, firms of similar character established in that town, and at the same time, also from Cheltenham, came S.E. Haywood a young mason who remained until 1947 when he took over the monumental business of J. and G. Lamb and 38 Sandford Street, then owned by F. Perry.

Between the years 1927 and 1929 an interesting intercourse took place between the Director of H.M. Office of Works at Westminster and Mr. J.H. Bridgeman regarding a proposal to effect a restoration of the stonework of the Houses of Parliament. The discussion, following an inspection of the building in May 1927, lasted over a period of two years after which a tender was submitted.

The argument in which a number of master-masons and architects, including Mr. Walter Tapper, together with the owners of the Stancliffe Quarry near Matlock had been involved was debated in the House on Wednesday 18.5.27 when Bridgeman's name was mentioned several times. Seemingly revolving around the weathering propensity of Stancliffe stone was against that of the existing Anston it was agreed on Bridgeman's recommendation that Stancliffe was entirely suitable, and further - interesting to note - the fear that the working of

Stancliffe was a frequent cause of silicosis was ruled out. The potential involved was considerable and regret was caused when the tender submitted by Mr. J.H. Bridgeman in 1929 was not accepted. (Incidentally W. Chatterton, working for others, later fell from the roof and was killed).

Mr. Walter Tapper, rarely seen at the works, was a man of austere appearance. In 1930 he was made an Associate of the Royal Academy of London and was afterwards knighted, a belated honour, received virtually upon his deathbed. Much work was executed for him at St. Stephen's Church, Gloucester Road, London; the Church of the Annunciation, Quebec Street, Marble Arch; and in addition to numerous other large orders at home and abroad many items of free-standing furniture were supplied to important churches including Westminster Abbey and York Minster. He died September 1935 when the business devolved upon his son Michael.

Mr. Charles Bridgeman, though often called away to help his father with the management was usually found exercising his skill as a craftsman on the Gallery having become proficient in the art of modelling and sculpture, and during the negotiations of 1927/29 was sent to the U.S.A. where during a six week tour he contacted many architects and would-be clients showing by photographic media examples of the work produced resulting in several orders. An extensive order for statuary at Washington Cathedral was received but later vetoed due to the Wall Street crisis.

Mr. Ernest Standley was now established in charge of the office intermittently aided by a flow of youthful aspirants. To record in detail the numerous who came and went would be irrelevant, but one deserves mention, this being Sydney Behnam, who from 1925 remained upwards of five years to become a loyal colleague, before removing to the office of the 'Bishop's Call' and later to hold a position of responsibility with the Diocesan Board of Finance, so retaining an interest in Ecclesiastical affairs.

1929 saw the commencement of the restoration of the old Cathedral Church at Coventry. This consisted initially of minor repairs to the stonework by a mason of the name Went, but was soon to develop into a major operation, and in 1931 John Forbes, a Scotsman and local mason took over, by whom much of the exterior fabric was restored, including tracery work in the windows and replacement of the ornamental parapetting for which John (Jock to his intimates) supplied templates. His system of setting out, described as 'lines huip' or 'lines doon', was not always understood , more than once stones being worked in reverse or upside-down. These errors, however, by some ingenious method of fixing, Jock usually contrived to overcome.

In 1936 alterations to the Sanctuary were commenced under Mr. W.H. Randoll Blacking, F.R.I.B.A., the Close, Salisbury. This involved the removal of the existing arcading, figure niches, corbelling, etc. of a previous restoration, and replacement by a plainer concept to bring back the structure as nearly as possible to its original appearance. During the process the old foundations were unearthed and later re-covered by the new flooring, but to retain archaeological interest movable slabs were arranged over the bases of the columns to enable inspection by visitors. The existing furniture was replaced too, including Bishop's throne, sedilia, communion rails, and pedestals in oak. The work was dedicated on the 21st April 1937. Other contracts, inclusive of the crypt and various of the chapels, were nearing completion at the outbreak of the Second World War, only to be destroyed in the great air raid of November 14, 1940.

The firm had not been immune from the depression that overswept the country. The national unemployment figure of 2,000,000 was reflected through the ledgers of the period, indicating a fall from 70 men at work in 1932 to 35 the following year, a number never again to rise appreciably. One regrettably made redundant was Charles Pilsbury, a young man with ten years experience as a draughtsman and promising in the art of heraldic decoration, a skill inherited from his father and grandfather, the latter mention in connection with the early restoration of the Cathedral.

While an effort to secure a potential order was being made, Mr. Harry Saunders, probably never before out of work, also experienced a spell of unemployment. The effort proving successful Harry was recalled, but remained one day only, the following morning the sad news of his sudden death being received which occurred on the 15th October 1935 at the age of 54.

At short notice the work was executed by Saunders' former under-study Eric Loach of Knowle who had also been 'stopped' but now returned and remained with the firm until scarcity of work and the imminence of another war caused him to change his occupation - the opportunity to join his father in a family business specialising in nuts and bolts, in view of the existing conditions, opening to him a better prospect. George Lowther having died in December 1929, Eaden Keyte, now sole survivor of the old school, and in future to divide his time alternating between the band-room and the gallery, when on the latter exploiting his latent talent as craftsman in wood, which he exercised until his retirement in 1947.

As the year 1937 approached, to keep those who remained happy, a number of small items for stock were invented bearing motifs relevant to the forthcoming Coronation of King George VI and Queen Elizabeth. These, together with garden ornaments in stone, small figures and other knick-knacks, were displayed and sold in the showroom that had been formed by reducing the area taken by the stores.

Mr. Bridgeman had also acquired the old cottage adjoining his property which he renovated to resemble as nearly as possible its original appearance of approximately 1555. This found work for the carpenters and provided more accommodation for his 'antiques'. Unwittingly the altered building was to become highly attractive to visitors and the lane one of the city's much photographed views.

But the days were not all lean. For those able to remain a flow of small orders 'kept the wolf from the door' while usually in some department a job of more substantial character would arrive supplied by one or other of the architects with whom the firm had kept in touch.

In 1939 under the guidance of Mr. W.H.R. Blacking a set of five figures in Caen stone were commenced to be placed in the vestibule of Salisbury Cathedral. These representing the saints; Osmund, Nicholas, Monica, Aldhelm and Francis, were modelled and carved by E. Keyte who considered them to be some of his best work.

Mr. P.B. Chatwin was a frequent visitor; and George Bernard Cox, a blustering personality but a good friend, was often seen on the premises. His work consisted mostly of contracts, including figure work in stone and wood, for Catholic churches in the district. An example is to be seen at Sutton Coldfield on the Church of the Holy Trinity erected by Messrs. J.R. Deacon of Lichfield, upon which the carved tympani over the main doorways were entrusted to Bridgeman's.

Occasionally a small order was received from Major J.C. Thompson of 21 Dam Street. Being the local diocesan architect this work was generally in the nature of repairs to residences owned by the ecclesiastical commissioners. Also from Mr. Harold Hughes, Diocesan Architect for Bangor, (though never seen on the premises) over the years many orders for free-standing articles were regularly received and despatched to various places in Wales. The names Llanallgo, Llanelian, Llanfflewin, Llanfairnghornwy, are remembered together with Dyserth, Bryncoes, Conway, Menai, and of course Bangor. In 1938 the Chancel screen at Clynog, near Caernarvon was restored, followed by work at Llandudno, Holy Trinity, inclusive of the marble floor and appropriate fittings in the Apsidal Sanctuary for Canon T.J. Rowlands. As evidenced by the following extract from a letter to Canon Rowlands dated 11.1.40 the death of Mr. Harold Hughes was deeply regretted -

"OUR FRIENDLY BUSINESS RELATIONS WITH HIM HAVE EXTENDED OVER VERY MANY YEARS"

- but the relationship was not entirely severed being continued with his associate Mr. W.G. Williams.

So upon this the second epoch of the firm's history approaching its conclusion, Mr. J.H. Bridgeman, like his father before him, could claim to have served the ecclesiastical and secular communities in all parts of the country, including, as just observed, a considerable amount of work 'exported' to the land beyond the border.

As well as those at Lichfield and Coventry the list includes the names of other cathedrals:- at Lincoln where a statue of the Virgin beneath the archway to the south porch was provided: Sheffield - a reredos for the side chapel all in alabaster inclusive of figures and decoration: screenwork at Manchester; and for the Cathedral churches of Birmingham, St. Philip; and Derby, All Saints, stonework and repairs.

Also it must not be forgotten that a quota had again been shipped overseas, retrospectively to All Saints Church, Trinidad, W. Indies; St. Joseph's, Harrisburg, U.S.A., St. Matthew, Hastings, New Zealand; while a further order about to be commenced for Napier, N.Z. was prevented by the disastrous earthquake that occurred there in 1931. And finally in addition to its normal routine, the firm was always 'on call' for maintenance for fabric on buildings in the vicinity and further afield, such as Powis Castle, Welshpool, where over the years numerous contracts large and small were carried out, - and this, in other spheres, for the next five years was to become a major part of the firm's activity.

CR80

WORKMEN OF THE 'MIDDLE AGES'

ST. MARY'S
CHURCH
BURWELL

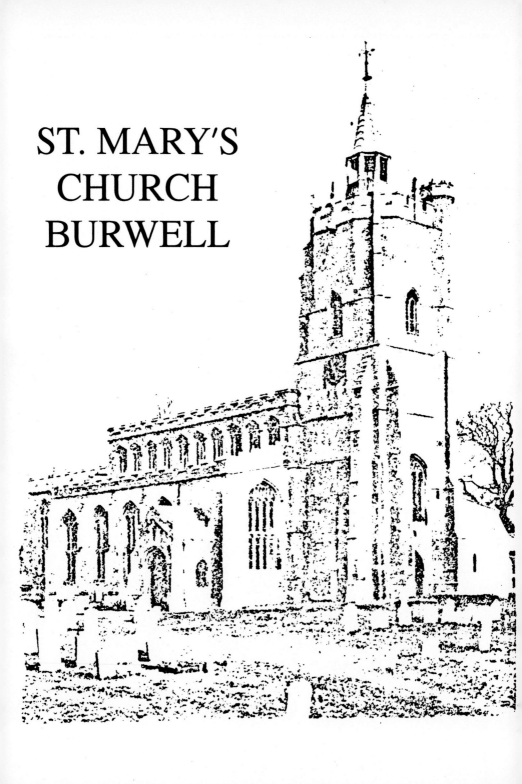

ROBERT BRIDGEMAN

THE CATHEDRAL RESTORATION 1876-1884

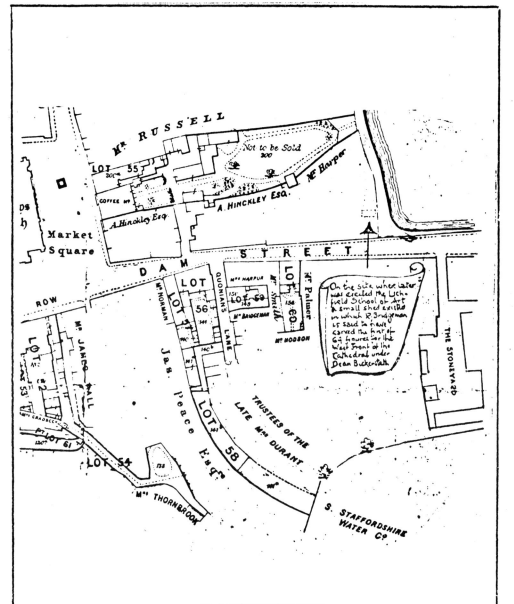

PLAN OF PROPERTY

MESSRS DANIEL SMITH, SON & OAKLEY

—— 1882 ——

(Historical Note and 'Stoneyard' added)

Dean Bickersteth 1875-92

Bishop Maclagan 1878-1891 afterwards Arch.Bishop of York

Dean Luckock 1892-1909

Bishop Legge 1891-1913

Bishop Woods 1937-53

Preb. Cresswell Vicar of S. Marys 1923-65

Dean Savage 1909-39

Dean Mellinger 1939-54

Dean Macpherson 954-70

Canon Kempson Custos 1937-1955

Canon Jenkins Custos 1955-60

Canon Robertson Custos 1960-64

THE CLERICS

'THE HIERARCHY'

JACK HAMLET
Great Grandson of the Master Mason

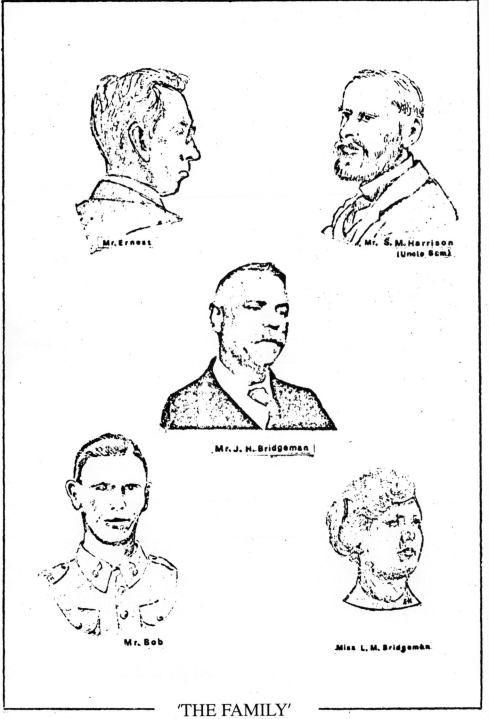

Mr. Ernest

Mr. S. M. Harrison
(Uncle Sam)

Mr. J. H. Bridgeman

Mr. Bob

Miss L. M. Bridgeman

'THE FAMILY'

SOME OF THE EARLY CRAFTSMEN
Sketched by E.K.

This Agreement setteth forth, That I Robert Bridgeman of the City and County of Lichfield agree with Mr John Keyte Relieving Officer of the said City, to take his Son William Eaden Keyte to teach him the Art and Craft of a Stone Carver For the term of Five years and seven months, From the seventh day of May One thousand eight hundred and Eighty seven to the nineteenth day of December One thousand eight hundred and ninety three. The said William Eaden Keyte then at the time of this Agreement being Fifteen years and five months old, And the said John Keyte agrees to pay to the said Robert Bridgeman the sum of Twenty pounds, Five pounds on the seventh day of May, One thousand eight hundred and Eighty seven, Five pounds on January first One thousand Eight hundred and Eighty eight, And the remaining Ten pounds on the thirtieth day of June One thousand eight hundred and ninety, And the said Robert Bridgeman agrees to pay to the said William Eaden Keyte Four Shillings per week for the first year and seven months, Five shillings per week for the second year Six shillings per week for the third year, Eight shillings per week for the fourth year and Ten Shillings per week for the last year. The Said Robert Bridgeman to pay in addition to the above sums, The travelling expences to and from, and allows Four shillings per week for Lodging of the said William Eaden Keyte at any job further than three miles away from the City of Lichfield.

Dated this Eighteenth day of July One thousand Eight hundred and Eighty seven

Signed by and in
the presence of each
other on the same
day

Robt Bridgeman
William Eaden Keyte
John Keyte

'LATTER DAY CRAFTSMAN'

'THE ENIGMA VARIATIONS'
Apologies to E.E.

MR C W BRIDGEMAN

R. BRIDGEMAN & SONS.
CRICKET CLUB.
JUNE 6 1914.

THE LINFORD WORLD

BRIDGEMAN   LINFORD   HILTON

THE COMPILER

THE
QUONIANS

INTERLUDE

O n the 4th September 1939 (the day following the declaration of the Second World War) sand-bags were filled and taken to the Cathedral to safeguard the choicest of the monuments, and almost immediately scaffolding was erected around the Lady Chapel to facilitate the removal of the famous Herkenrode windows. The involvement, constituting the safe preservation of one of the Cathedral's "MOST PRICELESS TREASURES", was capably carried out by Mr. Herbert Camm of Smethwick, a stained glass artist of repute, in association with whom the firm had worked on many occasions. All the panels, carefully numbered, were secretly deposited and stored in the nearby Anglesey Vault.

Of the craftsmen Charles Richardson a young joiner and N.C.O. in the local Territorial Force was immediately called away, while Alfred Bull re-enlisted and was given back his commission in his old regiment the South Staffords. The younger element, keen to go, were, by the Government's pre-arranged policy of selection, for a time mostly prevented. An exception was Arthur Sedwick working as a mason who volunteered to be early accepted in the Royal Engineers. Drafted to Crete, where he was posted missing, he became, so far as known, the first and only casualty. Atkins followed as a despatch rider, and later the woodwork department was to lose Whitehurst, Burnett, and Gardner, the latter joining the Navy as an artificer. At home Mr. C.W. Bridgeman and Mr. E.R. Standley joined the local defence unit in which Mr. Standley with previous war time experience became a platoon commander.

The phoney war period brought an order from the R.A.F. command to provide fittings in the temporary chapel at the newly erected camp at Hednesford, and also outstanding orders were being executed for Foleshill R.C. Church, Coventry, for Mr. G.B. Cox; and Nottinghill Gate, London for Mr. A.V. Heal, late Bodley & Hare. When completed these were duly despatched and fixed, but the two latter, owing to extensive damage by enemy action to the churches named were almost immediately dismantled and brought back to Lichfield to be safely stored throughout the war.

As the crisis developed, others took advantage of space made available by concentrating the smaller labour force into specific areas. Prominently the carvers' shop was vacated and utilised by the Birmingham Post & Mail to store their paper. Consisting of rolls, six to eight feet in diameter these were measurable in terms of miles. They were also very heavy necessitating the shoring of the floor.

The long expected break-through, with intensity of attack from the air, introduced a fresh dimension when a good percentage of the men who were left - labourers, carpenters, bricklayers, and carvers, were formed into a team and allotted an area in the Aston district of Birmingham, to which they travelled weekday and Sunday to effect first aid repairs to the damaged properties. Plumbers were added and the gang was put under the charge of Howard Russell, a good supervisor but not to remain long with the firm. These, financially though not enviably, were better off -Saturday (after midday) and Sunday (all day) being paid time and half and double time respectively. Curious entries in the wage book appeared some seemingly having worked 24 or even 26 hours in a day. This was a trick to save unnecessary calculations mostly applicable to Sunday activities.

Meanwhile at home, work of other national import was undertaken involving maintenance to premises under Government control inclusive of the local Post Offices, Telephone Exchange, Tanks and Transport (old Probate Court) Bird Street, and the Employment Centre, St. John Street; also at this time the Cathedral, Friary School, and other buildings, not forgetting the Johnson statue, to provide metal for war demands, suffered the loss of their boundary railings - being set in stonework this found employment for the masons. By this time J. Hamlet and D. Youngman had been called up, Jack to serve in France and Norway as a Paratrooper, and Don with the Artillery throughout the Italian campaign.

In line with schemes to relieve war tension Mr. Bridgeman made his premises available to the general public, who were allowed to enter and wander round at any time to see men at work on more peaceful pursuits. Among the many visitors attracted, those serving in the forces and parties of children from the surrounding schools were particularly welcomed. The idea was also to prove a means of advertisement, small orders being received from some who were admitted, and larger ones at a later date from certain whose interest had ensured for the firm a potential client, among them students at the local Theological College. Excelling at this period was Jimmy Clarke, a 'back-bencher' of the profession who had become the firm's only remaining mason and given work of higher quality to execute. This, including an intricately moulded memorial stone with stylish lettering, he undertook with relish. His quick wit (and temper) were well remembered. A khaki clad figure happening to stroll in on a day when the news was particularly bad was heard to remark, "You've go a big job on there, sir", to which Jimmy's caustic reply (ignoring the interest in his work) was, "Yes, and you've got a big job on too". His triumph was short-lived being overtaken by the complaint known as old mason (silicosis) to which he succumbed shortly before the war ended. Occasionally for short periods he had been assisted by his son Sammy when on leave from the army. Father and son were descended from the previously mentioned Sammy Clarke the blacksmith.

On July 16th 1942 a diversion occurred when the men were permitted to assemble at the lane end to see their Majesties King George VI and Queen Elizabeth drive by on their way from the Bishop's Palace to the Market Square, where Mr. J.H. Bridgeman was presented by Bishop Woods; and as Chairman of the Johnson House Committee had the honour of showing their Majesties over the birthplace of the Doctor.

The problem of blackout was overcome by devious means, and a fire-watching rota recruited that functioned until the formation of an organised street party. Also at the Cathedral extensive precautions were taken; a supply of water was effected by the erection of a 6 inch vertical pipe, installation of elaborate equipment, and a lookout post situated on the battlements of the central tower from whence the surrounding district could be observed. Here Mr. Charles Bridgeman with the Cathedral officials took his turn on the rota, but no incident occurred in which either team was involved.

Not so fortunate was John Forbes, who on the night of the 14th November 1940, together with the Provost and two others forming the guard for the night at the recently restored Cathedral Church at Coventry, was to witness the great incendiary raid on that city in which "MORE AND MORE (bombs) WERE SHOWERED DOWN, NEARER AND NEARER THE CATHEDRAL" until eventually one was seen to have "DONE WHAT WE MOST FEARED" (Provost's Account) having pierced the roof and ignited the woodwork beneath. Many more followed creating a situation powerless to control. By morning light Jock was to see the work of years, his own and that of his predecessors, a smouldering ruin.

In 1942 Whittington Barracks became the depot of the 10th Replacement Unit U.S. Army who during their stay presented new stained glass to take the place of the plain lights in the westernmost window of the Garrison Church. Mr. Geoffrey Webb of East Grinstead, Sussex, was chosen as the artist, the taking of all particulars and fixing being entrusted to Bridgeman's. For the erection of ladders etc., to make the preliminary survey a squad of G.I.s was provided commanded by a N.C.O. - a humorous though somewhat overwhelming experience. Vestment fittings were also executed and placed in the R.C. Chapel form them, an operation devised and directed by a corporal of the name Ted Hunt.

The difficulty of obtaining a suitable junior assistant for the office arose at this time and the position was eventually filled by one of the fair sex, Margaret Sanders, who remained until 1956 as a popular member of staff and first of a line of female helpers.

The work was not all sanguinarily motivated - in addition to trays for bread and other short supply items in demand at the time, orders for ecclesiastical supplies less expensive in character were obtained and sometimes a larger commitment. In 1942 the Convent Chapel at Haunton near Tamworth was provided with fittings; in 1943 work for both the R.C. and Parish Church at Cannock executed; and for Darlaston a substantial lychgate made and erected.

In 1944 the Children's Corner at St. Mary's Church, Lichfield was furnished inclusive of a two purpose altar, carved and decorated in mahogany incorporating a panel depicting Noah's ark haloed with the rainbow.

The conception of Mr. C.W. Bridgeman, the altar was made reversible to reveal at Christmas time a recess containing a crib. At the same Church in 1945 a new pulpit was erected, which with soundboard and connecting panelling was the design of Mr. F.H. Crossley of Chester (noted for his writings on medieval church woodwork) and ordered by the family of the late Alderman Andrews. Coincidentally the civic seats were installed as the joint gift of Mr. J.H. Bridgeman (then alderman of the city), his family; and Mrs. H. Russell in memory of her husband, a former town clerk.

The progress of the work was viewed with interest by the vicar, prebendary H.S. Cresswell, a frequent visitor to the works throughout his long incumbency of 42 years at St. Mary's.

As the war drew toward its close, a number of competitive trophies for the Borough of Oldbury Council were commenced. These, covering a wide field were embellished with motifs relevant to the activity depicted and provided work for designer, joiner, carver, and decorator.

It seemed evident when the fire-precautionary measures were unexpectedly lifted that the promised 'beginning of the end' had been reached, and, with the disbanding of all the civil defence units apparent that the cessation of hostilities could not be long delayed.

In May 1945, at the instigation of Sir Winston Churchill, Victory in Europe was celebrated with a two-day break, and similarly in August of that year, upon the collapse of Japan and the final surrender of all the opposing forces.

CB⊗O

THE AFTERMATH

T he welcome change from total war to total peace immediately brought a spate of enquiries and orders with which the firm was inundated, thus giving the lie to those prophets of doom who had pronounced Bridgeman's a luxury establishment and forecast its early closure. On the contrary the mundane activities that had served to keep open the doors throughout the crisis at once became subservient, and arrangements to meet architects, clerics, and others again became necessary. Before the end of 1945 the old haunts around Birmingham and the Black Country had been visited while early in 1946 journeys to outlying towns and villages within the diocese and beyond were being undertaken. These were often made difficult by depleted rail and bus services due to shortage of man power and rationing of petrol, but by devious means appointments were kept and rewarded with the receipt of the orders sought.

Conversely travel was economical, so far little advance being made on fares or accommodation. A typical outing to the Black Country embodying calls at Walsall, Wednesbury, Dudley, and Brierley Hill was made at an overall cost of 2s 8d. (13½ p) while St. Martins, near Oswestry and Gobowen at the extreme edge of the diocese was accomplished for 13s 6d (67½ p) Further afield still work was procured at:- Colsterworth, Lincolnshire, a singular feature of the building (once a leper hospital) being its sloping floor upon which a screen had to be arranged; at Tring, near Watford, Herts., where traditionally styled Altar Rails were installed; and St. Helens, Lancs., involving a contract for the successors of William and Segar Owen, Architects, Warrington, the total expenses of the latter visit of inspection, inclusive of bed and breakfast amounting to £1.6s.2d.

Simultaneously, as when the war commenced, so upon its conclusion, scaffolding was immediately erected around the Lady Chapel at the Cathedral; this time to return the coloured glass panels to the Herkenrode windows. Before re-insertion the temporary clear panes had to be removed and the original leaded lights repaired and cleaned, an operation again entrusted to Mr. Herbert Camm of Smethwick. When replaced the windows were floodlit from inside revealing to the passer by outside a spectacle not before witnessed and probably never to be seen again - this in vivid contrast to the darkness of the war years.

At the works some difficulty was experienced in obtaining material. A part of the large stock of timber had been commandeered while the remainder could be used only on permit, licensing being still in force. Labour was also a problem. The Government's policy of selection used at the outset to ensure an even flow of manpower now operated in reverse, those in the forces being but slowly released from service so that the ones at home accustomed to periods of short time found themselves working overtime.

James Maunder, having taken over from C. Pennington upon his retirement in 1937 and whose death occurred during the war, was in charge of the woodshop and had remained throughout. Assisting were George Boggis returned from Aston, and several youngsters, among them Bryan Knowles, Dennis Griffiths, Brian Lawrence and Derick Herbert whose uncle, the Rev. J.H. Herbert, Rector of Brierley Hill was a frequent visitor bringing some good orders to the designs of Mr. H.C. King, Architect of London.

Also welcomed back after a short absence was Mr. Harry White, a hard working carpenter from Walsall, who, with his assistant Horace, had been mostly engaged on constructional work, notably the Lychgate at Stony Stratford, Bucks., and more recently that for Darlaston, Staffs. Harry's oft repeated phrase 'the world's gone mad' and his adopted demeanour of domestic suffering as a hen-pecked husband and father of two accomplished daughters (of whom he was inwardly proud) are well remembered.

The death of William Bull, (Senr.), in retirement, had recently occurred and his sons, William, (Junr.), with Alfred following work of importance elsewhere, now returned to the carvers' shop to be joined by George Burnett and a young man of varying adaptability, Ron Walker. (Alf as an older man had been early released from his second spell of army life). Augustus Clarke was back on the Gallery with apprentice Harry Comley; while the joiners received Bernard Whitehurst and Charles Richardson, the latter from service in Burma as a commissioned officer.

Commencing in 1929 as a junior Richardson had become proficient in all branches of his trade including the art of french polishing. This he had learned from James Mapson upon whose premature death in 1937 he carried on as an able substitute. Clever at bending timber, prior to the war he built for Mr. C.W. Bridgeman a holiday caravan with all the necessary furniture and fittings, which, when not in use, was kept as a showpiece in the space below the carvers' shop. Named by Mr. C.W.B. 'The Mercian' it was eventually sold, all particulars having first been taken with intent to construct another on similar lines.

Presumably Richardson would have been employed to execute the new model but before a start could be made the offer of further service lured him back to the army where he remained for a number of years with the rank of captain, and afterwards held a departmental post in civilian capacity.

50

From the details retained a somewhat enlarged 'Mercian' was successfully executed by Leslie Phillipson, a young man with air ministry experience who came to the firm as a probationary in September 1945. The building of the caravan proved Leslie's capability, and in due course many responsible tasks, later to be mentioned, fell to his lot.

As after the first war, commitments necessitated the setting on of more staff. In the lower office a female helper for Margaret, and for Mr. Standley a colleague - Raymond, younger brother of Sydney Benham, from service in the navy, while the drawing office was augmented by Ian Woolford to work beside Derek Osburn who had commenced as a young boy in 1945 and remained to become a useful assistant.

It would be impossible and indeed superfluous to enumerate all the places and to chronicle all the work coming the way of the small band now returned to their former occupations, but none-the-less in this the third chapter of the saga the record would be incomplete if some mention were not made of the higher lights. Were the undertaking large or small the expertise was in no way diminished and sometimes it was that a smaller effort attracted more notice.

Over the years stemming from a commission in 1909, several small caskets to contain illuminated scrolls presented to certain honoured as Freemen of the City had been executed, and in 1945 at the instigation of Mr. J.H. Bridgeman a tablet bearing their names was placed in the Guildhall. Last to appear on the list was 'THE 10TH REPLACEMENT DEPOT U.S.A. FORCES' on whose behalf the Commanding Officer, Colonel J.A. Kilian received a casket by Bridgeman's constructed of oak found in the vicinity of Whittington and lined with wood from the bombed Houses of Parliament.

The interest of the citizens was duly evoked, and aroused even more upon the announcement that Bridgeman's had procured the order for a further piece of craftsmanship for presentation to one whose name had become universally famous and was to be similarly honoured elsewhere; the name was that of Field Marshal Montgomery then to be made a Freeman of the Berkshire Borough of Maidenhead. The casket in brown oak had upon its sides carved motifs depicting:- the town's seven arched river bridge; the crest of St. Paul's School where 'Monty' was educated; his private arms; and a hunting scene reminiscent of exploits with the Afrika Korps. On the lid was a plate inscribed with the wording:- "PRESENTED TO FIELD MARSHALL SIR BERNARD LAW MONTGOMERY, C.C.B., D.S.O., BY THE MAYOR, ALDERMEN AND BURGAGEES OF THE BOROUGH OF MAIDENHEAD ON THE OCCASION OF HIS ADMISSION TO BE AN HONORARY FREEMAN OF THE BOR-

OUGH 1945" and the whole was surmounted with a representation of the Field Marshal's baton.

Appropriately Mr. and Mrs. J.H. Bridgeman were invited to attend the ceremony; and later a picture appeared in the periodical 'ILLUSTRATED' of the Field Marshall at his home in Hampshire surrounded by his trophies, the Bridgeman casket clearly visible in the foreground.

Notwithstanding a depleted staff of masons, work at the Cathedral, unavoidably delayed, had at once to be recommenced. At the conclusion of the war S.E. Hayward was 'holding the fort' with two newcomers Bill and Len Potts travelling daily from Derby, and these were augmented in 1946 by Atkins released from the forces, George Green, and apprentices George Bannister, J. McClarren and T. Ottewell. Bert Portlock had returned to Cheltenham in 1932 and upon the death of Ernest Hamlet in 1940 and that of his brother Arthur soon afterwards no one was officially engaged as foreman until the arrival of Potts Senr. who acted the part until 1949, when Ernest's younger son, Jack, returned from the army, was given supervisory jobs away from home and became the obvious choice.

Sir Charles Nicholson's first major contract (post war) was the restoration of the north aisle windows and buttresses of Lichfield Cathedral. Completed in 1948 this also proved to be the last of Sir Charles' projects due to his retirement and death that occurred at a great age shortly afterwards. A recognition of his skill and that of the workmen appeared in the Lichfield Diocesan Magazine at the time compiled by Dean Iremonger an extract from which read as follows:- "IF YOU WOULD SEE HOW MUCH MORE SKILFUL OUR ARCHITECTS AND MASTER-MASONS OF TODAY ARE THAN THEIR FOREBEARS, STAND... ON THE SOUTH SIDE OF THE NAVE. FACING YOU IS A COMPETENT PIECE OF RESTORATION;... BUT WHAT HAS HAPPENED TO THE BEAUTY OF THE ORIGINAL? THEN TAKE A LOOK AT THE BUT-TRESSES ON THE NORTH SIDE... AND SEE HOW IT IS POSSIBLE TO RESTORE A BUILDING WITHOUT ROBBING IT OF ITS SOUL!... WE AND THOSE WHO WILL COME AFTER US, OWE A DEBT OF DEEP GRATI-TUDE TO SIR CHARLES NICHOLSON... TO MR. CHARLES BRIDGEMAN, AND TO THE MEN WHO CONTRIBUTED THE WORK OF THEIR HEADS AND THEIR HANDS IN THE STONEYARD AND ON THE SITE".

One of Jack Hamlet's first tasks under the new consulting architect Mr. George Pace of Clifton Green, York was the removal and renovation of approximately 19 feet from the apex of the central spire observed to be unsafe. First the erection of tubular scaffolding was required, a mighty task put into the experienced hands of W.J. Furse & Co., Steeplejacks of Nottingham and accomplished by their foreman J.A. Tinkler. This enabled an initial inspection by the architect and contractors and among the first to ascend to the ball were Mr. C.W. Bridgeman, J. Hamlet, and the writer of this history.

It was soon found that extensive repairs were needed to other parts of the fabric and with the scaffolding in position this was seen to be the time to effect an overall restoration including the renewal of badly eroded stones, the making good of fractured window heads and cills, repairs to tracery and weatherings, the replacement with delta bronze of all wrought iron bands, bolts, stays, etc., pointing of joints, rendering of friable faces to both spire and tower, together with a complete examination of the lightning conductor.

The major operation entailing the removal of the wrot'iron summit cross and copper ball (or orb) with the taking off of twenty-two tapering stone courses was successfully achieved by the steeplejacks which when lowered were brought to the Quonians and reared in the yard, the offending stones being replaced by new while the remainder were re-dressed ready for re-fixing. The cross was changed for one of gunmetal to a subtle design of the architect based on the Jerusalem motif found in the cathedral arms, while the ball (2ft diam.) was re-used, and the whole specially prepared and covered with two layers best double English gold leaf.

Executed in situ by the late Mr. George Kingsland of Birmingham, after twenty-eight years is still seen (1977) glittering in the sunshine, a testimony to his skill.

Relics of the previous restoration (1893) recovered from the ball were removed for preservation and replaced by a scroll inscribed with the names of those who then held high ecclesiastical and civic office, together with a record of the men who carried out the work; and, as a gesture of appreciation on the 19th of June 1950, a dinner was arranged by the Dean and Chapter who invited all the tradesmen to join them at the Swan Hotel. Among those who spoke after the Bishop (Dr. E.S. Woods) paid particular tribute to certain observed from his study window 'up in the clouds' whom he concluded could legitimately be termed 'high churchmen'. To foot the bill "NUMEROUS SUBSCRIBERS GAVE THEIR SUPPORT AND THE COST OF THE WORK AMOUNTED TO MORE THAN £9,000" - an enormous sum in those days but by later standards to become increasingly insignificant. (Illum scroll).

A few statistics will be of interest. The following table, based on a week of 46½ hours, is complied from the year books of the N.F.B.T.E. (National Federation of Building Trades Employers) to which the management with three other firms in the industry, were affiliated as a local branch and to whom Mr. E.R. Standley acted as secretary.

	CRAFTSMEN			Grade A	LABOURERS		
	Rate	Weekly Wage	Incr.	Grade A	Rate	Weekly Wage	Incr.
1940	1/8½	£3 9 5¼		"	1/3¾	£3 1 0 ⅜	
1941	1/10	£4 5 3	1½	"	1/5¼	£3 6 10 ⅛	1½
1942	1/11	£4 7 2½	1	"	1/6¼	£3 10 8 ⅝	1
1943	2/0	£4 13 0	1	"	1/7	£3 12 9½	¾
1944	2/1	£4 16 0½	1	"	1/7¾	£3 16 6 ⅜	¾
1945	2/1	£4 16 0½	0	"	1/8	£3 17 6	¼
1946	2/6	£5 16 3	5	"	2/0	£4 13 0	4
1947	2/9	£6 7 10½	3	"	2/2½	£5 2 8¼	2½
1948	2/9½	£6 9 9¾	½	"	2/3	£5 4 7½	1½
1949	2/10	£6 11 9	½	"	2/3¼	£5 5 7½	¼
1950	2/10½	£6 13 8¼	½	"	2/4½	£5 10 5¼	1¼

It will be noted that remunerations, virtually static between the wars, had now almost doubled, and while it was anticipated that a slump following the pattern of the post 1918 period must soon come, the flow of orders was not retarded, wages continued to rise, and prospectively the earnest of the MacMillan axiom "NEVER HAD IT SO GOOD" seemed on the way.

During the decade 1945 to 1955 much timber work, inclusive of small fixtures and free-standing articles, was provided at approximately four hundred places, all in addition to the work already mentioned, and contracts at some forty other places in the district where larger undertakings were executed.

It was also imperative that an amount of post war restitution be tackled.

The fittings prematurely despatched and hurriedly brought back from Nottinghill and Foleshill, since the fabric of the buildings concerned was repaired, could now safely be reinstalled, while at the same time under the direction of Mr. Philip Chatwin; the badly damaged furniture from St. Mary's Church at Acocks Green was renovated and renewed. At Earl Sterndale, an isolated church on a hill top in Derbyshire that had received a chance hit causing the destruction of all the seating, this was newly made and placed in the reconstructed building for the architects succeeding Naylor, Sale and Woore of Derby; and, for Mr. G.B. Cox, Birmingham stonework at St. Osburg's R.C. Church at Coventry involving the renewal of all the traceried windows badly damaged in the great raid of November 1940 found work for the masons.

Meanwhile, again at Coventry, John Forbes had been kept busy cleaning the debris from the 'nave' of the Cathedral Church in preparation for the completion of the new building. The clearance was a major operation, but upon the decision to commence the new edifice, regrettably little or no part of the work was entrusted to Bridgeman's, though, to anticipate, upon its consecration on Friday, 25th May 1962 in the presence of Her Majesty the Queen, a member of the firm was chosen to sing in the massed choir comprised of those of the surrounding Cathedrals. The singer was Peter Ward who in 1950 had commenced his career at the works as a woodcarver under Mr. Alfred Bull, and possessing a fine alto voice was appointed Vicar Choral of Lichfield Cathedral in 1958.

Peter's artistic ability, inherent of accomplished parents, soon led to other spheres, especially that of high class decoration in which he mastered the art of burnishing - the hardening of the surface of gold or silver leaf to enable the attainment of a gloss finish by polishing with an agate so giving the appearance of lustrous metal.

But to revert: among the many contracts for new work received was a vaulted screen for Linton, near Maidstone, Kent, A.V. Heal and R.V. Smith, architects - A finely embellished Baldachino and High Altar at the Church of St. Gregory, Bearwood for Mr. Philip Chatwin - complete fittings embodying panelling with battle honours and military insignia at the round church of St. Chad, Shrewsbury, for Mr. Bernard Miller, Principal of the Liverpool School of Architecture - and for the same architect, the renewal of all the furniture destroyed by a disastrous fire at St. Michael's Church, Tettenhall, Wolverhampton - all major undertakings and also, on the secular side, provision of new library fittings for King Edward VI Grammar School at Stafford.

It had been expected that the war memorial trade would again predominate, but in the event progress in other fields was not interrupted. Of the hundred or so commitments dealt with a fair percentage consisted of adjustments to existing tablets etc., to include the new names, that usually amounted to a third only of those previously inscribed.

As at Lichfield, the same technique was applied to outside memorials, and it would appear from the records that only one completely new monument was made, such being an elegant cross in Portland stone for Wantage, Berks., to the design of Frederick Etchells, responsible at the time for a quantity of work upon which artistic lettering was the main feature.

During the same period about 300 grave memorials for private individuals were provided, and to augment those in the stone shops the names Davies, Tidy, Hillman and Littleford appear - the two former of short duration, while the latter, at the commencement of their career, were to remain.

In the woodshop employment had been found for two good local men - Jack Walker and Bob Wakelin, also a Polish immigrant Bruno Skylenski, while due to his father's advancing years and debility Mr. Charles Bridgeman was virtually in control and ready when the time came to take over as boss.

Dying on the 24th February 1951 at the age of 80 Mr. J.H. Bridgeman had lived to see his son, sometime Councillor, made Sheriff of the City, the family being thus invested with a three-fold honour. Somewhat characteristically, Mr. J.H.B. at the time of his own shrievalty (1927) was the only member of the Council recorded as not fulfilling the office before wearing the Mayoral chain which he did in the years 1922 and 1923, a fact subtly recorded on the family memorial "TWICE MAYOR AND ALSO SHERIFF OF THIS CITY".

Present at the funeral service was his old friend W.E. Keyte not to know that on the same day at the same hour a week hence (Wed. Mar. 7) he was himself to be laid to rest having died on the 4th in his 80th year.

In 1947 when forced to retire through failing health he had completed 60 years without break in the employment of the firm becoming well known and well liked among his colleagues, and though of different religious persuasion respected by all, layman and cleric alike. Well remembered was his aptitude for producing lightning sketches of his workmates and others - often 'speaking' likenesses - some being used to illustrate these pages.

Upon assuming full control one of Mr. C.W. Bridgeman's first decisions due to excessive commitments and pressure on workmen and staff, was to take down the 'PLEASE ENTER' signs to which the public had become accustomed and whose interest had not flagged.

A visitor's exclamation 'more interesting than the Cathedral' among the workmen had become an oft-quoted catch-phrase and shortly following the closing of the doors, an order was received for work at a remote church at Edenfield near Ramsbottom, Lancashire. This came from the proprietor of a mill for the weaving of woollen fabrics trading as Thomas Aitkin & Sons Limited, and significantly was found to be the result of a routine visit to Lichfield during the war of the company's salesman, Jim Woodcock, who had responded to the Bridgeman invitation to 'walk round' and subsequently recommended that the firm's services be enlisted. The order, envisaged of simple nature, soon developed into a contract of some magnitude when the building was eventually refurnished almost throughout. Numerous visits were made to advise and take particulars, and as designs were submitted, an appeal to the employees was made for funds to defray a proportion of the cost, the owner (Mr. Dewhurst) to offset the balance. Upon completion the various items were collected and installed by the resident carpenter J. Salisbury.

In 1952 the family was again honoured when Mr. C.W. Bridgeman, following in father's and grandfather's footsteps was made Mayor of the City, adding to the figurative mantle inherited from his predecessors a triple distinction and though in this case the office was held for one year only, his term as Sheriff had by chance been prolonged to run from November 1947 to May 1949 covering the period of adjustment affecting all municipalities in those years. On both occasions the staff were invited to attend the inaugural ceremony at the Guildhall.

The commercial side of the Showroom was at this time being developed to encourage the sale of subsidiary requirements including communion wine, and on 31st March 1954 the firm was incorporated under the company act to become R. BRIDGEMAN & SONS LTD. whereupon the names C.W. Bridgeman* - G.L. Bridgeman were underwritten upon all letter heads.

The new regime was now to embark upon a further period of prosperity. In addition to architects and clients of the older generation other names began to appear:- Baines, Provis, Cope, Leicester; J. Tarney, Lancaster; Forsythe Partners, Shrewsbury; A.L. Linford, Tamworth; and locally, Warwick Scott, successor to J.C. Thompson, Diocesan Surveyor, Dam Street.

Previously well known as Major Thompson's assistant, Mr. Scott dealt mostly with dilapidations but often explored other fields resulting for the firm in the receipt of numerous orders. The premature death of Mr. Scott was regretted, when his diocesan work was transferred to the business of Wood, Goldstraw and Yorath, whose extensive practice at Tunstall enveloped the Potteries.

Nearer home, dating from 1905 the Bridgeman connection with the Black Country Church of St. Bartholomews, Wednesbury had become well known. An eminent landmark once dominating the woodlands of Cannock Chase, through-out the years in this building for the architect C.E. Bateman much work had been executed, not least the extensive wall panelling 'saturated' with incised and gilded commemorative inscriptions. Following the death of Mr. Bateman the order was received for the large screen that now adorns the entrance to the Chancel.

This was directly sponsored by the Vicar (Preb. A.B. Labelle later Precentor Lich. Cath.) to be designed and detailed by the author for Robert Bridgeman & Sons Ltd. The concept in English oak comprising ribbed and groined vaulting in the perpendicular style of the 15th century, was unique in that the side portions had to be arranged to form vaulted canopies over the earlier installed clergy seats and desks.

The work inclusive of intricate carving and tracery was accomplished under the

---

*Mrs C.W.Bridgeman

watchful eye of J. Maunder to the satisfaction of the donor and all concerned.

Another undertaking of outstanding merit was the execution in 1955 of an altar piece and elaborate screenwork to be placed around the apse of the R.C. Church of St. Lawrence at Birkenhead. In style imitative of the Gothic revivalist, Pugin, this was to the design of Messrs. Reynolds and Scott of Manchester, architects again new to the firm.

As at Wednesbury and Birkenhead many of the contracts contained carving and sculpture which, in addition to orders for individual figures and other ornamentation, kept the craftsmen busy sometimes demanding spells of overtime. Augustus Clarke having died in 1950, the brunt fell on Alf Bull, his brother William, and George Burnett; whilst in the absence of H. Comley, called away for his period of national service, the figure work was taken over by P. Conoley from Cheltenham assisted by a young man in the early days of his career, Denis Parsons.

The sculpture included representations of the Christ (crucified and in glory); a comprehensive range of saints and angels; a 3 foot figure of the Archangel Michael for shipment to Michigan, U.S.A.; and, among the miscellany, an amount of work from Messrs. Rattee and Kett of Cambridge culminating in repairs to the badly damaged High Altar at St. Paul's Cathedral, London. This consisted of fruit swags, scrolled consoles and cherub heads all carved in pine wood and overlaid with gold leaf in the style of Sir Christopher Wren.

At the instigation of the Government an element of foreign labour was introduced giving assistance in the joinery department - Max Cutayer of Egyptian origin and Martin Pataki-Istok a Hungarian. These were good workmen but the bilingual improvisations of the former were sometimes difficult of comprehension. In the lower office acting as receptionist and helping Mr. Standley, was Susan Williams, a young lady of artistic tendencies later to be exploited.

The workshops would sometimes be enlivened by the visit of an early associate - Edgar Harvey, in the early 20s a young apprentice carver, now a 'northcountry' journeyman, - Trevor Wright, police officer on leave from Rhodesia, - Fred Ollivier, prior to the war returned to his native Guernsey where he had survived the German occupation, - and on an even more nostalgic note, in January 1955 the visit following an absence of thirty-five years in Australia, of 'Orlando' better known in the 20s as 'Harry' Dutton.

Temporarily residing at Cheltenham Harry at once made the journey to Lichfield to be welcomed by those of his associates who remained at the works and to look round the old city.

Reminiscing on the past, his experiences in the art of modelling, painting, and sculpture had led in many directions, notably the execution for the Australian Government of a mammoth relief map of the country. Originally commenced for security reasons 'with the Japs on our doorstep' this was developed to become a faithful representation of the structure of the continent. The model roughly 30ft long and 30ft wide was made to an arbitrary scale of eight miles to the inch and is now on permanent exhibition at the University of Melbourne. Somewhat disappointed by the altered appearance of the old country Orlando eventually decided to return to the land of his adoption where he died in 1962.

Among others who had strayed was Jack's elder brother Richard (Dick) Hamlet, who, inclusive of military service had been away for 19 years but in 1955 returned to remain with the firm until his retirement. Commencing in 1925 as a boy of fourteen, in 1936 Dick had been forced to leave due to shortage of work - his role now became that of guiding the young element in the workshop leaving his brother free to supervise all outside labour.

It seemed almost that the wheel of fortune was turning full circle when the old name Rattee and Kett reappeared; but the year 1956 was to see an even fuller turn when, as in the early days, priorities became centred once more upon the Cathedral.

On September 27 of that year an appeal was circulated by the Dean (W.S. Macpherson) for £200,000, urgently needed "TO SAVE THE CATHEDRAL FROM DECAY AND RUIN". Included in his itinerary the Dean cited four items needing urgent attention - Woodwork, Stonework, Lighting, Heating, all of which directly or indirectly, would affect the firm that had so long helped to preserve and maintain the building.

Repairs to the fabric had become an unending occupation - here a little, there a little - as finance permitted, but the immediate task in the current crisis was that of restoring the woodwork and here Leslie Phillipson, introduced earlier, will step again into the narrative.

Routine inspection by the Architect, and Custos (Canon Jenkins) with Charles Bridgeman had discovered the ravages of the deathwatch beetle to be so widespread that much of the timberwork, to avoid collapse, must be immediately replaced. This entailed that the roof coverings, including all slating and leadwork be removed and carefully preserved for replacement.

Work was at once commenced on the north transept, but the first task was to clear the roof spaces of the litter of ages, mostly responsible being the jackdaws and pigeons that for generations had made the roof their home. Cart loads of debris in the form of twigs and branches from the surrounding trees, together with heaps of lime droppings had to be carried away, a task made difficult by the undulatory nature of the walking space, in shape the reverse of the vaulted ceiling beneath, the nooks and crannies having become the habitat of the birds.

This formidable operation under control, one could now tackle the main 'enemy'.

To eliminate the beetle it was necessary to cut out all powdered wood which in many instances meant the removal of an entire beam without disturbing the balance of the main structure that had weathered the storms of seven or more centuries. For replacements various of the hardwoods were used, and this, for the most part, heavy and bulky, had somehow to be manipulated into position from ground level, a job skilfully handled by Phillipson and his helpers. All woodwork, to avoid further 'attack' was sprayed with WYKAMOL preservative and treated against dry rot with MUROSOL. Those administering the preservative were provided with masks to prevent nasal irritation akin to a prolonged bout of hay-fever.

The inaccessibility of the area required that planking be arranged as temporary walks for wheeling barrows etc., from which was evolved the idea of the permanent gangways complete with handrails bridging the vaults that now stretch the entire length and breadth of the building; and whereas hurricane lamps, torches, or even matches were wont to be used to grope one's way, often on hands and knees, switches and light points at all strategic positions were provided by the electricians.

The large space in the great tower above the crossing of the nave and transepts was used as workmen's quarters where not only electric light but a mains water supply was installed - a boon to the masons when grouting in their joints, not to mention the many cans of tea brewed on the primus stove that someone had been inspired to provide.

The transept on the north side completed, next was tackled the chancel, and then, in order clearly remembered by Phillipson, the choir, south transept, nave, north choir aisle, south choir aisle, St. Michael's and St. Stephen's chapels, organ chamber, and library annexe.

The workmen employed under Phillipson consisted of carpenters: H. Marshall W. Eales, E. Round, Charles Hodson-Walker, former wheelright and undertaker; and interestingly, Peter Dakin, a great-grandson of one early recorded in the narrative as driver and maintainer of the old gas engine; masons: (in co-operation with J. Hamlet) G. Bannister and T. Ottewell, with labourer; A. Irwin, and bricklayer, W. Lee. This gallant company for ten years virtually 'lived' on the premises.

In addition to the gangways, much other essential woodwork was coincidentally executed:- the floor and ceiling of the room in the central tower (workmen's quarters pro tema) were repaired; and to keep out the ousted jackdaw, all louvres to the dormer windows were renewed or adapted to be fitted with wiremesh. Inside and out, making good the stonework followed displacement and replacement of plates and beams, and as each section was completed the roofing had to be reinstated all as before. This was proofed against fire and storm to the architect's specification: first was placed a layer of aluminium over all the rafters then upon vertically laid counter lathing, rolls of ruberoid upon which the main horizontals were fixed to receive the slates; and finally the asphalted gutterings and outlets, leaded flats, soldered flashings, and concrete work, a specialists job accomplished by Leslie himself.

At the office much clerical work was involved, adequately kept up to date by Ernest Standley, Ray Benham, and Susan, while at the receiving end, Canon Jenkins and others 'sought out many inventions' whereby to raise the enormous amounts required:- Deeds of Covenant; Illustrated Lectures; Garden parties; Sales of Work; Organ Recitals; Collecting Boxes; Coffee Sessions; waiving the newly passed 'act' a coffee morning and open day at the works was convened, and to augment the funds small crosses and silhouettes of St. Chad made from the surplus wood of the original beams were offered for sale. The state of the financial position was registered throughout upon a gigantic pseudo barometer placed in the Cathedral at the west end of the nave, but regrettably Canon Jenkins did not live to see the target reached or yet the completion of the work.

In 1962 the heating system was overhauled involving the change from solid fuel to crude oil. The boiler house below ground on the south side near the Consistory Court was re-sited and built above ground east of the Chapter House on the north side. An elongated oval in shape this was erected in stone and to save disturbing the chancel floor and choir seating, a means of communication between the two was arranged, via a cryptic passage that Phillipson claims to have discovered effecting considerable economy.

In 1964 a diversionary activity, though still connected, brought Leslie away from the Cathedral. To preserve the privately owned thoroughfare of the Close the legal requirement of stopping the way once a year had to be observed, and for the occasion posts stood at the western and southern boundaries with chains to draw across the road. Upon the annual event (mid October), Jack Martin and others, draped in sackcloth would be seen disconsolately performing the office of wardens, the weather by local tradition being mainly cold and wet.

Notices provided by Bridgeman's ('NO MOTOR COACHES' 'TRADESMEN ONLY' 'PRIVATE ROAD' 'NO HEAVY VEHICLES' etc.) were erected to no effect and eventually the traffic problem made necessary the decision to stop the right-of-way with a substantial bar-gate designed by Mr. George Pace and constructed by Phillipson which was placed at the boundary in Dam Street.

Back at the Cathedral the main cause for anxiety, by the efforts of Canon Jenkins enthused into the workmen, as being successfully removed, and with the conclusion of the work in sight, under the new Custos, Canon Robertson, the way seemed clear to pay attention to other outstanding necessities.

The inadequacy of the Choir Vestries had long been a subject of concern and it was decided the time had come to remedy this problem. First was involved a gigantic measuring operation from which a complicated survey was made for the architect to work out a scheme for the rearrangement of the existing accommodation covering the area, ground and upper floor levels, between the Vestibule and Chapel of St. Stephen. Eventually plans were received with the order to proceed and yet another seemingly impossible task was entrusted to Phillipson. Accepting the challenge with his usual optimism this proved to be Leslie's final triumph and when completed in 1968, his skill was acknowledged in visual form by a likeness head depicting himself in workman's cap with hammer on shoulder carved in stone upon a small turret at the northeast corner of the building.

The year 1968 was also to bring to a conclusion the final chapter of the Bridgeman story. But meanwhile, retrospectively within the compass of the decade up to 1965, those on the premises had been kept busy by a variety of activities. Again upwards of four hundred places could be cited for which contracts large and small were executed, all exclusive of the monumental trade responsible for the supply of some one hundred and eighty memorials.

Among the former were two substantial orders for work at Tipton, Staffs., and Ystradgynlais, S. Wales, coming from the successors of the long established ecclesiastical business of Jones & Willis, Birmingham, in process of being wound down by their principal, J. Parker, due to tenancy difficulties. Such were outstanding commitments and upon its closure the firm's albums of photographs and useful addenda were passed to Bridgeman's for safe keeping and future reference. Incidentally an estimate for the work at St. Matthew's, Tipton had been previously tendered by Bridgeman's but not accepted.

Several jobs of unusual character should be mentioned, notably the stall-work for the Priory of the Greyfriars at Oxford. Replacing furniture of traditional style, this, the conception of Mr. Fleetwood Walker of Birmingham consisted of miserere seating with canopied soundboards connected by plain upright boarding. Of modernistic design, the work featured a variety of material, including Afrormosa, Honduras and West African mahogany, with contrasting veneers of Indian laurel, Tasmanian blackwood, Madagascan ebony and English ash - a contract truly unique, both architect and style being new to the firm.

Back to traditional, at Salford Priors, Warwickshire, an ingenious design for a memorial tablet to Mr. Harry Evershed was received from the architect, P.B. Chatwin. Well known chairman of a reputed company of engineers and contractors for steam cultivation under the name Bomford & Evershed, the family arms surmounting the memorial was given as 'supporters' a steam roller and traction engine all neatly carved in Ancester stone. The failing eyesight of the architect, now virtually retired, necessitated that the drawings for his approval be very boldly rendered.

From time to time contracts of special artistic merit found their way into the itinerary, sometimes for architects practising in 'amateur' capacity - carved Tester at Chiswick for Lord Norton; elaborate covework at Easton Neston for Mr. Forsythe Lawson; and at Great Thurlow a small village bordering the counties of Suffolk and Cambridge, period screen work for Lawrence Bond, Esq., Grantham.

Duncan Steward of Liverpool, introduced Chancel fittings of modern design for Harlescott, Shrewsbury. At Manchester, Kensignton, and Weoley, work for Mr. Gilbert Scott (another apparent breakthrough but this Mr. Scott was found to have no connection with the original). At Mortomley near Sheffield, medieval styled choir seating, a Bridgeman conception by permission of Mr. George Pace, consulting architect to the local P.C.C.

And again items for export - the name Remiera, Aukland, N.Z., appears in the records; Vancouver, St. Chads; Rehoboth Beech, Delamere, U.S.A., Prince Town, New Jersey; Detroit, U.S.A., the already mentioned Michigan, U.S.A., and a further order for Hastings, N.Z., while of family interest, for St. Cyprian's School, Cape Town, name boards were supplied for Miss June Averill, daughter of Mr. C.W. Bridgeman's sister Mrs. L.P. Averill appearing early in the notes as Miss L.M. Bridgeman. To a bookshop in California two statuettes of Dr. Johnson were despatched, also at the Garrison Church, Fermanagh and Lisburn, Northern Ireland the provision of baptismal fittings.

So with the conclusion of the second post-war decade in sight, Mr. C.W. Bridgeman was able, as had his forbears, to look back, though in smaller compass, upon a period of further progress, and notwithstanding a somewhat altered personnel, unimpaired workmanship.

But the imminence of change was apparent:- in 1964 the replacement of Tory by Socialist administration followed by the devaluation of the pound; the substitution of V.A.T. for S.E.T; the ever rising cost of materials; unrestrained wage increments; impending inflation - such were the factors menacing the trade of all small concerns, and from the signs an approaching slump was again feared, one that would materially affect the sale of all articles of luxury.

Added was the position of Mr. Bridgeman himself who was now nearing the normal retiring age, with no foreseeable successor, his son, Robert, though a qualified architect, having had no connection with the business. Also it was to be expected that Bridgeman's keyman E.R. Standley would soon be contemplating retirement.

About this time, visits of certain unfamiliar to the premises were observed, leading to curiosity and speculation, and indeed negotiations were afoot, the sequel of which was soon to be made known. But meanwhile the work had to proceed, not least that involving the edifice and its environment around which the firm had functioned for so many years, and one of the last duties to be performed concerned the well being of its inhabitants.

The Cathedral Close, like the city, had originally its own supply of water, derived from springs at Pipe on the Maple Hayes Estate. The system dating from 1293 consisting of 2 inch lead pipes, at intervals repaired and renewed by similar of cast iron, followed a line through Pipe Green and adjacent fields and gardens to cross Beacon Street opposite the Cathedral approach road which it traversed to a supply tank and control box at No.15 on the north side of the Close.

Subsequent to the closure of the business of C.H. Salford, water engineer, Lombard Street, the upkeep of the whole apparatus became the responsibility of Bridgeman's when the oft-time emergencies were taken care of, in his own whimsical way, by Harry Gilbert, late of Salford, and to whom the firm and given employment in 1939.

During the ploughing season an annual episode was the severing of a section of the main, which due to a dip in the ground stood 'higher' than the remainder, the ensuing leakage and failure of supply causing annoyance and concern to land owner and householder respectively.

In 1946 with Harry's guidance, a complete survey was made and all details plotted on copies of the ordnance survey, following which, L. Phillipson, proficient in the art of lead workmanship, took over to successfully maintain the system until the end of its existence.

In 1930, by way of augmentation, a branch had been established from the town mains which involved the Conduit Lands Trust and frequent visits of their engineer, F. Lawrence, and in turn the source from the city's springs at Aldershaw, came to be augmented by the S.S.W.W. Co., who eventually took complete control, and finally (1968), the impossibility of retaining an adequate supply from those at Pipe having become apparent, harnessed the whole system to their mains.

Thus a historical link of 675 years duration was broken, an event that coincided with the retirement of Mr. C.W. Bridgeman, and the completion of the third chapter of the Bridgeman saga following 90 years of service to the ecclesiastical authorities, an important factor of its final phase, having been to ensure that the 'water of life' reached the inhabitants dwelling beneath the shadow of the Cathedral walls.

It was therefore with regret, albeit relief, when in early December 1967 the announcement was made that the firm was to be taken over by Messrs. F. & E.V. Linford, Building Contractors of Cannock, with the stipulation that all Bridgeman's employees would, or could, be found jobs and that the business would be carried on under the old name, and under the old roof, of R. Bridgeman & sons, Ltd. as a subsidiary of the larger firm.

By a happy circumstance it became known that those taking over though obviously larger of dimension were in descent from one CHARLES LINFORD who had started his own small business as a builder in Cannock in the year 1877 almost coincidental in date to the business established by ROBERT BRIDGEMAN in Lichfield.

Developed as a company in 1925 by brothers Fred and Victor Linford this in 1932 had been registered under the directorship of the forenamed and a third (A.C. Harborow) as F. & E.V. Linford Limited.

At the time of the takeover, though the name style F. & E.V. had remained, Ernest Victor had seen fit to set up on his own and eventually emigrated to Australia so leaving Mr. Harborow - Mr Fred being away from home at the time - to overlook the extensive alterations prospectively imminent.

CജBO

THE NEW WORLD

As the year 1967 drew to a close, apart from Cathedral maintenance, among orders being executed was a meticulously designed font in Portland stone complete with oak cover for the church of St. Peter, Virginia, U.S.A. By this the firm had been introduced to G. Robert Dukes, Esq., a schoolmaster of Stourbridge, Worcestershire, better known in the States for his architectural interests where he was acclaimed 'professor'. Not only was this contract virtually the last to be seen through by Mr. C.W. Bridgeman, but the first of a flow of commissions sponsored by Professor Dukes, later to be dealt with under the old name within the frame-work of the new management.

Of more urgency however, as the new year approached, was the making of a complicated survey of the band-room and office block needed for planning the proposed alterations tentative to signing the deeds appertaining to the takeover.

The latter being accomplished behind closed doors on Friday afternoon of the 16th February it then became known that Bridgeman's employees would be working side by side with those of the long established local building firm of Messrs. J.R. Deacon, the rear of whose premises in Lombard Street had for many years bounded that of the Quonians and whose small works department, upon the closure of the main company in 1967 had been taken over to continue in similar capacity under the auspices of Messrs. Linford.

The terms of the agreement were thus mutually convenient to Mr. Bridgeman (for reasons stated) and Mr. F. Linford, the company's chairman, in that the lease of the premises in Lombard Street was due to expire.

At the Quonians work commenced immediately. Early on Monday morning February 19th a gang of workmen arrived suitably equipped to tackle the formidable task of reconstruction, all to be completed for occupation by the new staff and workpeople within the short space of six weeks.

Briefed by Mr. A.J. Rock, manager elect, Ken Arnold, foreman; with labourers, carpenters, plumbers, painters and decorators; commenced the operation of pulling down and building up.

First, many of the models and casts, a feature well known to those within and without the city, had to be removed from their racks in the band-room - and worse, destroyed, among them the full size prototype of the King Edward VII statue given to the city by Robert Bridgeman in 1908, a work of art still to be seen in the Museum Grounds.

Simultaneously the clearance of the room abridging the band-room, for long used as a store and latterly combined with a cubicle for communion wine and candles, was being effected. When cleared the whole was lined with celotex boarding and prepared to receive the drawings and records later to be brought from the Bridgeman archives. Eventually this was efficiently accomplished, bundle by bundle passed from hand to hand by human chain and placed upon the original shelving also transferred.

The taking away of the fitments surrounding the apparently small room where the drawings had been kept at once transformed it to a large two-windowed apartment, and, occupying a central position, was chosen by Mr. Rock as his managerial office. The books and negatives were then taken from the adjacent 'library' to the new archives, enabling this to be used by his secretary.

Demolition advancing below, dimensions could now be taken and calculations made for the erection of an undercarriage required for the necessary extension on the upper floor. this consisted of three 8" x 6" upright stanchions upon which the R.S.Js (11" x 6") were to rest and subsequently the timber joists, boarded floor, and studding for walls and ceilings.

The former, accomplished under K. Arnold's supervision, Alan Silvester and carpenters quickly followed to build the additional accommodation, which, for the time being, provided a place for quantity surveyors; a ladies room; and small drawing office to replace the existing large room also in process of demolition.

On the ground floor, prior to a complete renovation of offices and showroom, all the furniture, shelving and contents had to be removed, sorted and dispersed.

More carpenters then appeared with hammers, nails, saws and stacks of celo' to square up and line the rough walls and ceilings. At the same time Gilbert Cooper and mate were assessing the heating situation; Grif (T.A. Griffin) electrician rearranging the wiring and light points; and Bill the bricklayer taking up and replacing the floor to the foyer and reception area.

Demolition of the stone stairway had also commenced while plans were being drafted for the erection of a new staircase of oak. Work on this was somewhat hampered as by now the drawing office had been reduced to carnage - the only means of reaching the upper floor being an upright ladder at the position of the old darkroom also demolished.

Even the inner sanctum (Mr. C.W. B's private office) did not escape. Here the 'museum pieces' - valuable samples of marble, photographs of ancient work, including those of the Deansgate Library at Manchester, together with pictures of R. Bridgeman and family were deprived of their places of honour. Not only had the room to be diminished in importance but reduced in size that a passage be formed with an opening at its end to effect at once alternative entry from the band-room and way through to the casting place where yet another office was to be arranged.

A further innovation was the provision of a small kitchen with sink unit and cooking appliances for staff meals. Taking the place of the stores (latterly a miniature compartment beneath the Gallery stairs) obstructed the existing entrance to the band-room from the office, but the doorway was retained as access to the new kitchen. The telephone cubicle, now redundant; was also removed, the space beneath the new staircase being reserved as a cupboard for cleaning utensils. All that survived was the strong room with built-in safe and metal door.

Meanwhile, the band-room had become a hive of activity. From its role of sanctity over many decades, this was in process of conversion to the mundane, the whole area now to be utilised as a mammoth store room.

To it shelving from Lombard Street, together with that of the Quonians and other available fixtures were being transferred and re-assembled. Renovation to the floor was in progress - some of the wood blocks were replaced with concrete, while near the entrance a small office was constructed for the storeman and the approach spanned by a wide counter with opening flaps.

Back in the offices the glaziers had been busy making good damaged window panes and replacing the old opaque glass with clear lights.

Next the paper hangers were on the scene lining the walls and ceilings, on their heels the painters and getting in the way, but welcomed 'coldly', the heating engineers fitting new radiators. Overall the whirr of drilling had to be endured, everywhere holes were being bored for the installation of the new telephone system throughout the premises, while lastly frantic efforts to complete were made by those laying lino on all the floors.

Keeping a watchful eye on the proceedings, throughout the operation frequent visits were made by Mr. A.C. Harborow, Vice Chairman of the company at Cannock, and when the day arrived to move in, all but minor finishings had been accomplished. On Friday March 28 the office furniture from Lombard Street arrived and on Monday April 1 1968 ('L' day) the 'Invasion' took place. So ended an epoch in which the work force had functioned expeditiously ten to twelve hours daily, weekday and Sunday for six weeks, an operation pronounced by Mr. F. Linford, just home from his winter visit to New Zealand - 'a good job of work'.

During the last week the ever willing Rene Austin was to be seen busily scrubbing the floors, dusting the files, polishing the desks, and not least, making tea and coffee against the day of arrival of the new staff. The geography of the place, always mystifying to strangers, now had to be relearned and the names of the incomers correlated. In various clerical capacities occupying the former Bridgeman drawing office now divided into two rooms were Mr. Alan Rudge, F. Gillett, J. Milner, P. Upton, and Joan, while opposite was the small newly formed drawing office, and adjacent a room for the surveyor David Ducie. To efficiently conduct the secretarial duties came Betty whose name, Mrs. B. Larkin, was posted on the door of the small oriel windowed room that had housed the Bridgeman library.

Below, Pauline the third female member of staff, held the position of receptionist manipulating the intricacies of the new office communication system, while the old casting place - cum stoke-hole, also transformed, was allotted to the supervisors, where could be found, when at home, N. Marsh, L. Robinson and J. Fisher.

The private office, reduced in size, was to become an interview room but initially remained a place for Mr. Bridgeman - (on the new letter heads described 'Associate')- and Mr. Standley for a short while to stay in advisory capacity.

Upon being taken over, all working for the old firm were retained.

These consisted of:

Masons: V.J. Hillman, T.N. Ottewell, G.F. Grimley, G.J. Illidge, R.J., R.H., and E.J. Hamlet.

Sculptor: D.A. Parsons

Joiners: K.M. Johnson, B.J.W. Hodson, L. Ingram, D. Youngman

Carpenter and Cathedral Supervisor: L. Phillipson

Machinist: A.E. Martin

Labourers: H. Marshall, P. Dakin, P.S. Jones, K.S. Garratt

Driver: A.H.W. Simpson.

To these from Messrs. Deacon's, inclusive of those working on the transformation, were added a number of tradesmen that was to bring the total to approximately 70 workmen though a good percentage, engaged on outside commitments, were not frequently to be seen on the premises. Among them was Albert Littleford who from 1961 had been employed by Deacon's but now returned to follow his previous occupation of masonry with his former colleagues.

For obvious reasons a new element had superseded the older generation - L. Dawson had retired followed by J. Maunder, and upon the death of G. Boggis in 1962, Don Youngman (who after demobilisation found employment with

Deacon's) came back to take over as joinery foreman. The carvers were denuded of the Bulls, William and Alfred, the latter in retirement from May 1963, while the sculptors lost P. Conoley, whose reign had been of short duration, and H. Comley, leaving Denis Parsons to succeed to the hierarchy of his predecessors.

From the office in 1966 the sad loss by illness and death of Raymond Benham occurred; and in December of that year, Susan, responding to the call of modern art in which she was later to be distinguished, also departed.

Jack Martin's long hard-working career had terminated with retirement in 1962 leaving Ted his brother as the longest working member on the firm while A.H.W. (Bill) Simpson coming as driver and labourer in 1954, under the new regime was promoted storeman.

And that 'time and change are busy ever' was also apparent from without, names long familiar to the records were no longer seen nor yet their owners in person. Mr. George Bernard Cox visited the works no more; in 1961 the accidental death of Lord Norton (alias Major Adderly) in a riding mishap was announced; and shortly afterwards, in old age, that of Mr. Philip Broughton Chatwin occurred.

The temptation to elaborate must be avoided except for the latter, the association of whose family with that of Bridgeman having lasted throughout the firms existence. In early days carved features in stone, without which no building of the Victorian era was complete, were executed in and around Birmingham for Mr. Julius Alfred Chatwin by Robert Bridgeman. The scope also covered church architecture, inclusive of projects at Edgbaston; Birmingham St. Philips, and elsewhere, in which Mr. J.A. Chatwin's son, Philip, undergoing training at the Birmingham School of Architecture and in his father's office was most interested. Upon his father's death in 1907, Philip succeeding to the practice, brought to Bridgeman's many orders, becoming well known to the workmen whom he was pleased to call his friends. Also a keen archaeologist P.B. Chatwin's advice on matters of restoration was frequently sought. Contact with the name is still maintained through his nephew, Mr. Anthony Broughton Chatwin, whose prowess inclusive of many excellent designs for church woodwork are remembered - to wit the organ panelling at St. Martin's, Birmingham, and the entrance porches at Tutbury and Brierley Hill - and latterly, the restoration of the stonework to the fifteenth century doorway of the Alms Houses known as Milley's Hospital, Beacon Street, Lichfield.

In days gone by other members of the Chatwin family acted for Messrs. Bridgeman in legal capacity.

Meanwhile under its new management concentration on the stone trade was envisaged as a more productive prospect, and estimates for restoration of

National Trust properties at Arbury Hall, Nuneaton, and Swynerton Hall, the Potteries; being accepted, followed by the renewal of the colonnading for Tamworth Town Hall, adequate employment for the combined staff of masons was found. At the same time the woodworking department, somewhat diminished in scope, received an unexpected boost in the take-over by Messrs. Linford of another small company trading as 'Hilton Cabinet'.

In charge came Roger Bents to whom, with Paul Hazlehurst as assistant, was given the position of joinery manager to supervise all timber work appertaining to Linford's Lichfield branch and its now two subsidiaries. This involved Bridgeman's men in the production of furniture of modern design, augmenting that of their own traditional style, a craft which as occasion demanded, they still pursued.

The necessity soon arose to increase the office staff and among several newcomers Derek Osburn, with experience elsewhere, returned. Also the need for more accommodation became apparent and certain changes were made including the restitution to its normal purpose of the recently vacated drawing office, which, though reduced in size, still provided more space and a better outlook for the occupants.

Meanwhile negotiations for purchase of additional property consisting of the old stabling and coach-house facing the yard were pending, which upon completion in 1974 provided extra garage and storage space while the area above made possible a further enlargement to the offices forming a compartment each for the cashiers and comptometer operators. This again involved adjustment to the wiring and heating. Just prior to Jack Martin's retirement in 1964 the labour of stoking the fires had been eliminated by the change from coke to oil fuel fed to a new boiler enclosed in a brick surround erected upon the site of the old engine house in the mill, made to heat successfully the premises both old and new. Dying in 1968 Jack did not live to see the metamorphosis.

Also the mill and workshop over were reconstituted, while the yard, side and rear completely cleared, became a parking place for private cars and the firm's transport, each section having its own fleet of vehicles.

The main company settling down to daily routine could now add to its general building activity the architectural expertise of Bridgeman's with that of the Hilton craftsmanship in the manufacture of contemporary woodwork; and while continuing to function in their own sphere using their own name, if called upon, each was able to assist the other, the stonemasons usually cooperating with Linford while the joiners, with less traditional work in view and reduced in number, merging with Hilton.

The latter, specialising in shop-fittings, school furniture, and crematoria, soon became involved with Linford's in security projects appertaining to bank premises and upon these the Bridgeman element has successfully adapted itself - on the bench in the manufacture of counters, cash-points, screens, etc. and in many parts of the country, mostly at weekends, fitting and fixing the necessary gadgetry to offset the intruder.

But this has not superseded the peaceful role. On the contrary craftsmanship in the old tradition still finds its way to the premises to be executed in stone, supervised since 1975 by Albert Littleford; in wood by Keither Johnson; and both by Denis Parsons keeping alive the firm's reputation as sculptor and carver of figures.

During the post take-over years, in spite of the new dimension, much ecclesiastical work has been accomplished - latterly stone and woodcraft at Tenby, S. Wales; alterations and fittings at Llanymynech near Oswestry; and for the palace of Westminster, watchmen's boxes artistically designed by the consulting architect.

An order for a large Lychgate for the Church of St. Andrew, Bordesley, Birmingham, was also (1978) to be put in hand, while a further enquiry through the old business of Rattee and Kett, Cambridge, for work at Westminster Abbey was being considered.

With the approach of the years 1978/9 it seemed fitting that some memento to perpetuate the Bridgeman saga over a century of time be placed on record hence the foregoing treatise made possible from the extensive records still extant, memory, hearsay, personal observation, and, where details have been obscure, a little licence. Apology must therefore be offered for any error, omission, or interpolation that may inadvertently have occurred while the thanks of the compiler are due for help received from individuals including the effort of Betty and Lynne in laboriously typing the script.

There remains now but to summarise the present situation and future prospect.

Within the period of this final episode it was inevitable that further change and loss by death must occur and included in the obituary are:-

1972, James Maunder, age 93, retired ten years. 1974, A.E. Martin, fifty-eight years service, retired two years. 1977, Lewis Dawson, 84, retired fourteen years, and, of nostalgic interest, Joseph Drew at Ipswich age 80.

In August 1975 the death of Mr. George Pace, 26 years Consulting Architect to the Dean and Chapter was announced, and the appointment in March 1976 of Charles Brown of Leamington Spa confirmed. Also in 1975 Mr. Bridgeman resigned his position of Surveyor to the Dean and Chapter a position inherited from his father. His periodical inspections of the fabric were recognised by the presentation of a silver salver at the Chapter meeting on October 10 inscribed "CHARLES BRIDGEMAN WITH GRATITUDE FROM THE DEAN AND CHAPTER 1975".

On July 4 1977 the death took place of Mr. A.L. Linford well known Church architect of Tamworth (brother and father respectively of Mr. Fred and Mr. David Linford, Chairman and General Manager of the Company). His friendly visits to the premises are remembered with esteem.

The year 1975 saw the departure of J. Hamlet to join his sons in a business previously commenced: also his brother Dick, followed in 1976 by D. Youngman, joinery foreman, and A.H.W. Simpson, storeman, all to retirement.

Finally, 1st April 1978, the following were the names appearing on the Bridgeman roll of employees:

Sculptor and carver: Denis Parsons
Masons: V. Hillman, B. Furber, K. Upton, E. Knight, B. Hutchings, T. Elson, M. Painter (a), M. Lamb (a), M Hathaway (a), S. Lea (a), T. Vaughan (a).
Joiners: K. Johnson, R. Davies, J. Baskerville (a).
Machinist: A. Nightingale
Labourers: D. Murray, G. Workman
Painter: T. Walker (son in law late J. Martin)
Driver: P. Smith
Supervisors: L. Phillipson (Carpentry), A. Littleford (Masonry)
Wages Clerk: Margaret Day

(a) = apprentice.

From the foregoing when the year 1978, that of the firm's centenary, approached it was observable that few of the old hands, certainly none whose names had been familiar throughout then remained. Many had passed from the scene while others with similarity of skill had taken their place. These during the final decade of the story, working beside those labouring in other spheres of activity having successfully met the challenge, at the same time upholding their own special branch of the profession, it now seems reasonable to believe the high standard of workmanship set by ROBERT BRIDGEMAN, emulated by his son JOSEPH and perpetuated through his grandson CHARLES, will assuredly be kept alive with the interest of Messrs. F. & E.V. Linford in the old Cathedral works at the Quonians, Lichfield now trading, under the guidance of Mr. David Linford at LINFORD BRIDGEMAN LTD.